Preparing for the Next Financial Crisis

In the years since the subprime financial crisis of 2007–2011, we have learned a number of important lessons about the crisis, and have subsequently applied appropriate legislation, such as increased capital ratios and systematic stress testing, in order to combat it. However, it would be naive to suggest that such measures have put an end to the possibility of future crises. In this book, senior figures in economics, risk management and the banking sector use active research and policy debates to offer a wide perspective on what the next financial crisis may look like and what can be done about it from a regulatory point of view. By first exploring issues of macroeconomic policy, and then studying cutting-edge methodologies, challenging important aspects of testing financial practice, this book will be an essential read for all those studying and researching financial crises, financial regulation and macroprudential policymaking.

ESA JOKIVUOLLE is Head of Research at the Bank of Finland since August 2017. He is also affiliated with the Department of Finance at Aalto University. In 2012 he was closely involved in the background team assisting Governor Erkki Liikanen when the report by the High-level Expert Group on reforming the structure of the EU banking sector (the Liikanen Report) was being prepared. He has published articles in several well-known academic journals and chapters in books on risk management. He is a member of the Council of Management of SUERF.

RADU TUNARU is Professor of Finance at the University of Kent Business School. He has published more than sixty articles to date and is the author of *Model Risk in Financial Markets* (2015). He has received six best paper awards, and his latest work includes three papers on real-estate derivatives with Nobel laureate in Economics Robert Shiller. He previously worked for Bank of Montreal and for Merrill Lynch, where he was a VP in Structured Finance. He served as an associate editor for *Journal of Portfolio Management* and *Journal of Banking and Finance*.

Preparing for the Next Financial Crisis

Policies, Tools and Models

Edited by

ESA JOKIVUOLLE
Bank of Finland

RADU TUNARU
University of Kent, Canterbury

CAMBRIDGE
UNIVERSITY PRESS

CAMBRIDGE
UNIVERSITY PRESS

University Printing House, Cambridge CB2 8BS, United Kingdom

One Liberty Plaza, 20th Floor, New York, NY 10006, USA

477 Williamstown Road, Port Melbourne, VIC 3207, Australia

314-321, 3rd Floor, Plot 3, Splendor Forum, Jasola District Centre, New Delhi - 110025, India

103 Penang Road, #05-06/07, Visioncrest Commercial, Singapore 238467

Cambridge University Press is part of the University of Cambridge.

It furthers the University's mission by disseminating knowledge in the pursuit of education, learning and research at the highest international levels of excellence.

www.cambridge.org
Information on this title: www.cambridge.org/9781107185593
DOI: 10.1017/9781316884560

First published 2017

A catalogue record for this publication is available from the British Library

Library of Congress Cataloging in Publication data
Names: Jokivuolle, Esa, editor. | Tunaru, Radu, editor.
Title: Preparing for the next financial crisis: policies, tools and models / edited by Esa Jokivuolle, Radu Tunaru.
Description: New York: Cambridge University Press, 2017. | Includes bibliographical references and index.
Identifiers: LCCN 2017034652 | ISBN 9781107185593 (hardback) | ISBN 9781316636534 (paperback)
Subjects: LCSH: Finance – Government policy. | Risk management. | Banks and banking. | Investments.
Classification: LCC HG173. P74 2017 | DDC 339.5–dc23
LC record available at https://lccn.loc.gov/2017034652

ISBN 978-1-107-18559-3 Hardback
ISBN 978-1-316-63653-4 Paperback

Contents

Figures

Tables

Notes on Contributors

Timotej Homar, works at the European Central Bank (ECB) in the Risk Analysis Division of Banking Supervision. Before that he was at the Macro-Financial Policies Division of the ECB. His research interests are in banking and corporate finance. In particular, his research focuses on intervention measures of governments and central banks during systemic banking crises. He received a PhD at the University of Amsterdam in 2016.

Seppo Honkapohja, D.Soc.Sc., is Deputy Governor of the Bank of Finland. He has been a member of the board since 1 January 2008. Dr Honkapohja is responsible for the Bank of Finland's scientific research and currency supply. When the governor is unable to attend, Deputy Governor Honkapohja will be his alternate at meetings of the Governing Council and General Council of the European Central Bank. Dr Honkapohja joined the Bank of Finland from the academic world. He was Professor of International Macroeconomics at the University of Cambridge in 2004–2007. His prior career included work with the Academy of Finland, University of Helsinki and Turku School of Economics and Business Administration.

Esa Jokivuolle, is Head of Research at the Bank of Finland since August 2017. He is also affiliated with the Department of Finance at Aalto University. In 2012 he was closely involved in the background team assisting Governor Erkki Liikanen when the report by the High-level Expert Group on reforming the structure of the EU banking sector (the Liikanen Report) was being prepared. He has published articles in several wellknown academic journals and chapters in books on risk management. He is a member of the Council of Management of SUERF.

Heinrich Kick, is currently working as supervisor in the Risk Analysis Division at the banking supervision department of the European

Central Bank (ECB), where he has previously worked in the Financial
Stability Directorate and the European Systemic Risk Board. Before his
career in central banking, he also gained private sector work experience in asset management at Sal. Oppenheim, specialising in strategic
asset allocation. His research interests lie in the field of macro-finance,
empirical asset pricing and systemic risk, and he has also conducted
policy-related studies, notably on the result of the ECB stress test,
the drivers of forbearance lending and changes in regulatory capital
requirements for securitisations.

Thomas Noe, is the Ernest Butten Professor of Management Studies
at Saïd Business School and an expert on corporate finance and corporate governance. His work has influenced the way companies are
financed through the issuance of securities, contributed to the way
we analyse systemic risk for firms and provoked a re-evaluation
of the way senior managers are compensated. He is one of the
twenty most prolific researchers in leading finance journals since
the turn of the century, with his research appearing in journals such
as the *American Economic Review, Journal of Finance, Journal of
Financial Economics, Review of Economic Studies* and *Review
of Financial Studies*. Currently, he is a co-editor of the *Journal of
Economics and Management Strategy*. He has served on numerous panels, programme committees and editorial boards, including
the board of the Review of Financial Studies. He is a professorial
fellow at Balliol College and a research associate at the Oxford–
Man Institute and the Centre for Corporate Reputation at Oxford
University, and the European Institute for Corporate Governance.

Huw Pill, is the chief European economist and co-head of the Economics
team in Europe. Based in London, he serves on the Macro Research
Operating Committee. Dr. Pill joined Goldman Sachs as a managing
director in August 2011. Prior to joining the firm, he worked at the
European Central Bank, where he was Deputy Director General of
Research and head of the Monetary Policy Stance Division. Earlier, he
worked at the Bank of England and at Harvard University, where he
was an associate professor of business administration. Huw earned
a BA in Politics, Philosophy and Economics from University College,
Oxford, in 1989 and an MA and PhD in Economics from Stanford
University in 1990 and 1995, respectively.

Adrian Pop, holds a PhD from the University of Orleans, France (December 2005). In 2006, he was awarded the prize for the Best PhD Thesis 2006 in Banking & Monetary Economics awarded by Banque de France. He is currently Senior Lecturer in Banking and Finance at the University of Nantes. From 2008 to 2013, he acted as economic advisor to the French Prudential Supervision Authority (Banque de France). He is the head of the Executive MBA Program at the Institute of Banking & Finance (University of Nantes). His main research interests include banking regulation and supervision, early-warning systems, Basel Capital Accords, market discipline, capital standards, pro-cyclicality, subordinated debt, credit spreads, credit ratings, stress testing in banking, market efficiency, informational content of security prices, contagion, credit derivatives, Too Big To Fail in banking, financial crises, Islamic banking and finance and corporate governance in emerging economies.

Lucrezia Reichlin, is Professor of Economics at London Business School, Non-Executive Director of UniCredit Banking Group, Research Director at the Centre for Economic Policy Research and Chair of the Scientific Council at the Brussels-based think-tank Bruegel. She served as Director General of Research at the European Central Bank (between March 2005 and September 2008). She is a co-founder and director of Now-Casting Economics Ltd. She is a columnist for the Italian daily paper *Il Corriere della Sera*. She received her PhD in economics from New York University and has held a number of academic positions, including Professor of Economics at the Université Libre de Bruxelles. Professor Reichlin has been a consultant for several central banks around the world, including the Board of Governors of the Federal Reserve. She has been Chairman of the Centre for Economic Policy Research (CEPR) Euro Area Business Cycle Dating Committee and was co-founder and scientist in charge of the Euro Area Business Cycle Network. She is a Fellow of the British Academy, a Fellow of the European Economic Association and a member of the Council of the Royal Economic Society. She is also on the advisory board of several research and policy institutions around the world. She has published numerous papers on econometrics and macroeconomics. She is an expert on forecasting, business cycle analysis and monetary policy. The econometric methods she has developed for short-term forecasting (now-casting) are widely used in several important central banks around the world. Her papers have appeared in top scientific journals, including the *American Economic Review, Review of Economic Studies, Review of Economics and Statistics, Journal of Econometrics, Journal of Monetary Economics* and *Journal of the American Statistical Association*.

Carmelo Salleo, is Head of Stress Test Modelling at the European Central Bank (ECB), a unit in charge of developing top-down stress testing models for macroprudential and supervisory purposes. Since 2014 he was Head of the Macro-Financial Policies Division at the ECB, a unit which, together with national authorities, developed an analytical framework for macro-prudential policy. In 2010 he joined the European Systemic Risk Board Secretariat as Adviser, in charge of coordinating analytical support to financial stability oversight and macro-prudential policy in the EU. He was previously Head of Unit in the Bank of Italy's Monetary and Financial Policy Department, dealing with the role of financial flows and the relationships between the real and financial sectors in the Italian and euro area economies. He started at the Bank of Italy in the Banking Supervision Department as Economist, in 1995. He holds a PhD in Economics from Harvard University.

Juha Tarkka, is Adviser to the Board at the Bank of Finland, advising the governor on strategic issues and organizational development. He was previously Research Supervisor and Head of Research (1996–2004) at the Bank of Finland. Dr Tarkka has published several scientific papers on monetary policy and macroeconomics. He is also one of the two authors of the two-volume official history of the Bank of Finland, published in 2011–2012, as well as the author of a Finnish university-level textbook on money and monetary policy. He served as president of the Finnish Economic Association in 2005–2006. Juha Tarkka has a PhD degree in Social Sciences (economics) from the University of Helsinki, where the topic of his dissertation was the pricing of bank deposits.

Radu Tunaru, is Professor of Finance at the University of Kent Business School. He has published more than sixty articles to date and is the author of *Model Risk in Financial Markets* (2015). He has received six best paper awards, and his latest work includes three papers on real-estate derivatives with Nobel laureate in Economics Robert Shiller. He previously worked for the Bank of Montreal and for Merrill Lynch, where he was a VP in Structured Finance. He served as an associate editor for *Journal of Portfolio Management* and *Journal of Banking and Finance*.

Jouko Vilmunen, is a professor of economics in the University of Turku. Earlier he was the Head of Research at the Bank of Finland. He has also worked as a national expert for Finland in the European Commission. Jouko received his PhD in economics from the University of Helsinki in 1992.

Nir Vulkan, is Associate Professor of Business Economics at Saïd Business School and Fellow of Worcester College, both at the University of Oxford. He is a leading authority on e-commerce and market design, and on applied research and teaching on hedge funds. Dr Vulkan is the author of one of the leading texts on the microeconomics of e-commerce, *The Economics of E-Commerce: A Strategic Guide to Understanding and Designing the Online Marketplace.* The book analyses online trading mechanisms and the way in which web-based technologies such as bidding elves, smart agents and shopping bots influence the behaviour of consumers and retailers. He received a BSc in Mathematics and Computer Science at Tel Aviv University and a doctorate in Economics at University College, London, where he was awarded the Dean Scholarship for excellence in PhD studies. Dr Vulkan became a lecturer at Bristol University in 1997, and in 2001 moved to Saïd Business School. He was the director of the Oxford Centre for Entrepreneurship and Innovation (OxCEI) and the co-founder and director of OxLab, a laboratory for social science experiments, both at Saïd Business School.

Larry D. Wall, is the executive director of the Center for Financial Innovation and Stability (CenFIS) in the research department of the Federal Reserve Bank of Atlanta. CenFIS was created to improve knowledge of financial innovation and financial stability and the connection between the two. Dr. Wall joined the financial structure team of the Bank's research department in 1982 and was promoted to executive director of the CenFIS in 2013. In addition to pursuing his research agenda, he leads CenFIS's activities, including its newsletter, *Notes from the Vault,* and conferences. He also provides policy advice. A certified public accountant, Dr. Wall is on the editorial boards of the *Financial Review, Journal of Financial Research, Journal of Financial Services Research, Journal of Financial Stability,* and *Review of*

Financial Economics. He is also on the Academic Advisory Panel for the International Association of Deposit Insurers. He is a past president and chairman of the trustees of the Eastern Finance Association. Dr Wall has also been an adjunct faculty member of Emory University and the Georgia Institute of Technology.

Introduction

ESA JOKIVUOLLE AND RADU TUNARU

Financial markets have become one of the most important areas of economic activities in developed countries. Trillions of dollars are traded on these markets and financial risks are diversified to a larger pool of investors than ever before. The benefits of these highly lucrative and sophisticated markets are overshadowed from time to time by spectacular crashes and crises. Many times, the financial markets have the capacity to regenerate and continue as if very little happened. Some other times, the crashes lead to crises and the crises spill over to the real economy. When that happens, there is a wave of criticism against banks and financial markets and a new wave of regulatory legislation is passed to fix the situation such that these crises should never occur in the future. Yet, in spite of increased regulation crises seem to recur again and again.

Crises seem to be different every time and there is no regularity as such, although problems seem to recur in certain asset classes such as real estate. The equity crash of 1987 was followed by the fall of the sterling pound in 1992, then the Asian crisis of 1997 and the Russian default of 1998 that led to the collapse of Long-Term Capital Management (LTCM), the first gigantic hedge fund. Then we had the dot.com crisis at the beginning of the 2000s and finally the series of crises that started in 2007. One regularity suggests itself: when severe banking problems are involved, the real economic consequences tend to be bigger and more enduring.

At the time of publication of this book we are confronted with very low, even negative interest rates, stagnation, deflationary pressures in some regions, political risks and Brexit. These can hardly be called normal times, and are to a large extent a legacy of the most recent crises. The future looks perhaps even too interesting for academics, and anxiety has been spreading out in many places. This may be the beginning of a new realism in finance and banking and many of the old norms may need to be reconsidered.

Although it is imperative that we analyse the most recent crises thoroughly, we hopefully do not miss the risks of the *next* possible crisis before they grow too big. Almost by definition, the materialisation and timing of a crisis are unpredictable, at least well in advance, because otherwise measures would apparently be taken to stop the crisis from happening. What we should do, however, is to better understand and identify dangerous developments that increase the likelihood of a major crisis, and take measures to reduce that likelihood early enough.

In the aftermath of any event many people know what we should have done to prevent the event, but that may be of limited help when preparing for future events. We may need to spend more time to look forward and try to prevent the next crisis if possible. To that end we need to create better tools to monitor the prevailing situation in order to chart a wider range of problem scenarios. Perhaps academics and experts in financial economics should spend more time 'indulging in controlled fantasies, trying to dream up new ... phenomen(a) that (are) not contrary to our knowledge, but perhaps beyond our experience', to borrow the adapted words of a famous physicist.[1]

This book outlines the discussions that took place during a one-day workshop organised in September 2015 by the Kent Business School at the University of Kent in the United Kingdom in close collaboration with the Bank of Finland. In that workshop various specialists debated on what could be and how we can prepare for the next financial crisis that may hit financial markets and economies worldwide. The chapters included in this book present macropolicy issues, stress testing issues, experimental finance and model risk views that may help regulators, policymakers, risk managers, academics and general practitioners in becoming more aware of the sources, channels and modes of manifestation of the next financial crisis.

Our view is that it is highly unlikely that financial crises could be eliminated completely, although we should be able to reduce their probability. Being better prepared also means better crisis management: that we can act quicker to deal with problems and avoid larger losses that would ultimately fall on the entire society. Neither would it be realistic to claim that this book covers all possible angles. The Brexit

[1] Excerpted from the libretto of the opera *Doctor Atomic*, written by Peter Sellars.

result highlights this, very little being mentioned during the workshop about this possibility and what it would mean. So, our scope is not to pretend we have a crystal ball or that we know what is coming next but rather to emphasize the diverse character of the next possible crisis scenarios. We promote learning from the past but also looking to the future and we advocate tool building and collective thinking about the problems emerging in financial markets.

It was our aim to bring together experts from a wide range of areas involving finance, policymakers, chief economists of investment banks, central bankers, academics and regulators from the United States, United Kingdom and European Union. We hope we have started a useful dialogue that should continue more regularly.

The book is structured in two parts. The first part comprises more policy-oriented views while the second offers a few analytical studies from a 'financial stability laboratory'.

Part I starts with Chapter 1, 'Non-Standard Monetary Policy and Financial Stability: Developing an Appropriate Macrofinancial Policy Mix' by Lucrezia Reichlin (LBS) and Huw Pill (Goldman Sachs). Focusing primarily on the European Central Bank (ECB)'s post-crises monetary policy, they consider the potential risks of central banks' non-standard policies for financial stability. They suggest a useful taxonomy of the different types of balance sheet policies and the types of financial stability risks to study these questions. They argue that central bank intermediation which substitutes for private intermediation during a crisis tends to bolster financial stability. By contrast, central bank asset purchases aimed at reducing returns on safe assets and thereby pushing private investors to longer term and higher risk investments may generate financial stability concerns. This can be the case if a flat yield curve puts pressure on banks' profitability, although the flat curve can also discourage maturity transformation. They conclude by pointing to the current discussion concerning the appropriate policy mix – comprising conventional and unconventional monetary policies, micro- and macroprudential policies, as well as fiscal policy – which could help achieve the aims of monetary policy without risking stability.

In Chapter 2, Seppo Honkapohja (Board member of the Bank of Finland) first discusses the various financial market developments that led to the most recent crises. Thus this chapter also serves as a

useful prelude to many of the themes developed later in the book. As
the title of his chapter, 'Financial Innovation and Financial Stability',
suggests, one of the key lessons from the crisis is to understand the
linkages between seemingly beneficial financial developments and the
risks they generate. He then provides a concise account of regulatory
reforms in Europe. Considering some of the same issues that will be
discussed further in Chapter 4, he concludes by discussing the challenges facing post-crisis macroeconomic research in its pursuit to better incorporate financial factors and to guide future macroprudential
policy making.

In Chapter 3, Larry Wall (Federal Reserve Bank of Atlanta) reviews
'Post-Crisis Changes in US Bank Prudential Regulation'. He also offers
some comparisons with the corresponding European reforms (which
Seppo Honkapohja discussed in more detail in Chapter 2). Wall argues
that in many cases the new regulatory rules adopted by the United
States largely as part of the Dodd–Frank Act have been stricter than
those required by the international agreements. The United States has
also taken additional measures that are not required by international
agreements. On the other hand, Wall notes that as a result of differences
in the US generally accepted accounting principles (GAAP) framework, the largest US banks report significantly higher regulatory leverage ratios than would be the case under the International Financial
Reporting Standards (IFRS), the accounting framework used in the
European Union. Europe has also adopted stricter regulations on
bankers' variable compensation than the United States.

In Chapter 4, 'Financial Markets and Policy through the Lens of
Macroeconomics', Jouko Vilmunen (Bank of Finland) reviews the
state of macro modelling in the wake of the crises. He focuses on
the Dynamic Stochastic General Equilibrium (DSGE) models, which
have over the years become the 'workhorse' modelling framework for
central banks in particular. He considers the criticism these models
have encountered in the wake of the crisis, and takes a constructive
view of how to move forward. Continuing the work on incorporating financial frictions in these models will be the key, but that may
not be enough, given the current limitations of the DSGE framework.
Alternative modelling approaches including smaller and more partial
models will also be needed. A constructive 'dialogue' between the different modelling approaches is also necessary.

Part I ends with Juha Tarkka's (Bank of Finland) fascinating historical perspective on regulatory ideas on how banks should invest, titled 'Investment Doctrines for Banks, from Real Bills to Post-Crisis Reforms' (Chapter 5). He shows how thinking in this area has evolved over time with a varying emphasis on liquidity and solidity of bank assets. The emphasis has changed as a result of developments in central banking and the growth of money markets. According to him, attention shifted from liquidity, which the real bills doctrine emphasized, to the solidity of collateral. As a result of the *anticipated income doctrine* of banking and the idea of liability management, liquidity considerations were displaced by credit risk management and capital adequacy. However, the latest crisis has forced a reconsideration whereby the liquidity of bank portfolios is again emphasized.

The second part is dedicated to what may constitute tolls in a financial laboratory that may improve our knowledge of how crises appear and what to do to capture early signals about them.

In Chapter 6, 'Stress Testing in Banking: A Critical Review', Adrian Pop (University of Nantes/Nantes-Antlantic Economics and Management Laboratory LEMNA) revisits the main theoretical underpinnings of the various stress testing methodologies used by the main central banks and prudential authorities, highlighting the macroprudential lessons learned thus far. In addition, a rigorous and practically flexible new methodology for stress testing is revealed that is aiming to detect 'extreme but plausible' economic scenarios, using statistical techniques proven to be capable of detecting outliers in macroeconomic time-series data. This new methodology infers the shocks endogenously, circumventing the ad hoc approach used in the literature and practice so far.

Chapter 7, 'Making Sense of the EU Wide Stress Test: Comparing SRISK and the European Central Bank/European Banking Authority Measures of Bank Vulnerability', by Timotej Homar (ECB and University of Amsterdam), Heinrich Kick (ECB and Goethe University Frankfurt) and Carmelo Salleo (ECB) is also dedicated to stress testing. The authors present a practical comparison of the SRISK approach and the ECB/EBA method to assess stress test results through the lenses of capital shortfall. They found significant differences between the two stress measuring methodologies, with the ECB/EBA measure being driven by bank credit losses and bank vulnerability while the

SRISK measure used largely in the United States being driven mainly by the banks' leverage ratios. Their conclusions point to a direct relationship between SRISK stress impact and market leverage ratio, which may explain the discrepancies between the SRISK and ECB/EBA approaches in particular for banks that are on their way to bankruptcy and also for banks that are extremely well capitalised.

In Chapter 8, 'The Role of Personality in Financial Decisions and Financial Crises', Thomas Noe (Said Business School, Oxford University) and Nir Vulkan (Said Business School, Oxford University) use a psychological laboratory style of investigation to track down the role of personality traits as contributors to the behaviour of financial actors. The ultimate aim is to assess the effects of personality on aggregate economic outcomes. Their research shows that personality variables may play a significant role in predicting economic behaviour. Furthermore, they also reveal that personality had a strong impact in group decision context while being insignificant in individual decision contexts. This is an area of research that will attract no doubt intensive research in the immediate future, with a focus on integrating the personality variables into a general economic framework for decision making.

Part II ends with 'Model Apocalypto' Chapter 9). In this chapter Radu Tunaru (University of Kent) presents a critique of the model development process in finance. The field of finance, being intrinsically an empirical science, requires robust inference tools. Models are the primary tools of knowledge discovery but the rate of their production seems to increase exponentially. It is argued that more models will not necessarily improve knowledge in finance. Lack of understanding of models' capabilities and pitfalls contributed to huge losses in the banking system. He argues that the lack of understanding of models applied in the financial sector may generate a significant crisis in the near future.

The book is aimed at academic specialists, practitioners and professionals in the field of finance and financial markets. The volume should be attractive to regulators, risk managers, economists at financial institutions and central banks, journalists, investment bankers and hedge fund managers covering macro event risk, as well as academics and postgraduate research students working in finance and risk management areas.

We would like to thank Cambridge University Press, and in particular Phil Good, for helping us to bring this volume to light.

We are also indebted to several people who provided their support in organising and running the event in Canterbury. To this end we would like to thank Kimberley Attard-Owen, Jagjit Chadha, Catherine Lucas, Ian Marsh, Roman Matousek, Martin Meyer, and Paul Verrion for all their good will.

1 | Non-Standard Monetary Policy and Financial Stability: Developing an Appropriate Macrofinancial Policy Mix

HUW PILL AND LUCREZIA REICHLIN

> An ultra-accommodative monetary policy brings with it long-term risks to the stability of the financial system. First, because of the mounting risk of financial market bubbles, ... [and] second, because profitability in the banking sector can take a hit.
>
> Dr Jens Weidmann, president of the Deutsche Bundesbank[1]

1.1 Introduction

Central bank balance sheets in advanced economies have expanded significantly since the onset of the 2007–2009 financial crisis. Faced with market dislocations and the threat of deflation, all the leading central banks have engaged in non-standard monetary policy actions (such as quantitative easing, credit easing, liquidity injections and forward guidance) in an attempt to contain the crisis, revive economic activity and stabilise the outlook for price developments.

Yet such non-standard measures are understood to come with risks which are larger than those associated with the standard monetary policy practice aimed at lowering the target short-term interest rate.

Initially, the rapid expansion of central bank balance sheets associated with the adoption of various non-standard policy measures was seen to portend inflation risk.[2] But, at least thus far, inflation has failed to materialise. On the contrary, despite an ongoing expansion of both the European Central Bank (ECB)'s and Bank of Japan's balance sheets, concerns in Europe and Japan remain centred on downside risks to price stability

---

[1] See Weidmann (2016).
[2] See Meltzer (2009), A23, which contains the sentence: "The enormous increase in bank reserves – caused by the Fed's purchases of bonds and mortgages – will surely bring on severe inflation if allowed to remain."

(and deflation), rather than on inflation. Even in countries that are more advanced in their recovery (the United States, the United Kingdom and – within the euro area – Germany), price and wage developments have been persistently and surprisingly weak. In most macroeconomic forecasts, the global inflation outlook remains benign across the advanced economies, with risks to the downside rather than the upside.

Nonetheless, concerns about the pace and magnitude of central bank balance sheet expansion endure. But these have shifted away from inflation towards worries about financial stability.

In this chapter, we argue that not all central bank balance sheet expansions are the same in this regard. Allowing central bank intermediation to substitute for private intermediation when markets seize up tends to bolster financial stability.[3] By contrast, asset purchases aimed at reducing returns on safe assets and pushing private investors further along the risk and maturity spectra than they would otherwise choose to go may have an ambiguous effect on financial instability risks.

Unlike with a traditional reduction in the policy rate, which is associated with a steepening of the yield curve, active central banks' purchases of longer term government securities have a flattening effect on the yield curve. As a consequence, these policies squeeze financial institutions' profitability, which may raise concerns about the effect this has on their capital. On the other hand, a flatter yield curve reduces the incentives for banks to engage in maturity transformation and therefore makes these institutions safer.

Therefore, even abstracting from the beneficial effects that balance sheet policies have on aggregate demand, their effects on financial stability depend on a variety of factors: the 'active' or 'passive' nature of these policies and the way in which financial intermediaries respond in their balance sheet management, which in turn depends on their business model and the characteristics of the financial sector.

1.2 Two Rationales for Central Bank Balance Sheet Expansion

In the academic monetary policy literature, non-standard central bank measures have been based on two broad motivations.[4]

---

[3] See Giannone, Lenza, Pill and Reichlin (2012).
[4] See Lenza, Pill and Reichlin (2010) and Pill (2010). A third motivation is often also highlighted, although it remains something of a legal and institutional taboo: supporting government financing. In the euro area, non-standard central

1.2.1 Complementing Standard Policy by Supporting Conventional Transmission Channels

One set of measures aims at maintaining the normal channels of monetary policy transmission, from interest rate decisions to price-setting behaviour. By their nature, such non-standard measures are natural *complements* to the conduct of conventional monetary policy. The two elements work together: unconventional tools act to maintain the transmission of conventional instruments in what would otherwise be difficult circumstances.

Viewed from this perspective, central banks provide support to the private sector through non-standard measures at times of stress, so as to maintain the functioning of financial markets, institutions and infrastructure. In essence, the central bank acts as a 'central counterparty of last resort', facilitating trades that are necessary for the operation of the wider financial system (and thus for the economy as a whole) that the private market can no longer intermediate. The expansion of the central bank balance sheet – as larger monetary policy operations on the asset side accompany an accumulation of excess reserves on the liability side – is typically one outcome of such support.

In the euro area context, one prominent example of such a measure was the introduction of fixed rate/full allotment tender procedures at the ECB's monetary policy operations in October 2008 (Figure 1.1) at a time when the private interbank money market had seized up owing to concerns about bank default risk following the failure of Lehman Bros. In mid-September,[5] the ECB acted as a de facto central counterparty, replacing interbank payments via private intermediation that were no longer possible.

Not only did such actions contain and ultimately reduce money market spreads (Figure 1.2), but by maintaining interbank flows these actions were crucial in preventing other market malfunctions and ultimately had a more significant impact on credit flows, economic activity and the outlook for price developments.

---

bank policy measures – in the form of sovereign asset purchases by the ECB – have created 'fiscal space' on government balance sheets, allowing easier fiscal policies than would otherwise have been the case.

[5] See Heider, Hoerova and Holthausen (2015), who propose a model of adverse selection in the interbank money market to explain the seizing up of private intermediation in this period.

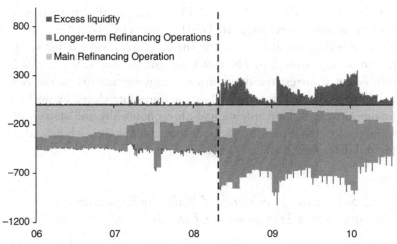

Figure 1.1 ECB non-standard measures (in EUR bn.) facilitate central bank intermediation of money market transactions.
Source: ECB

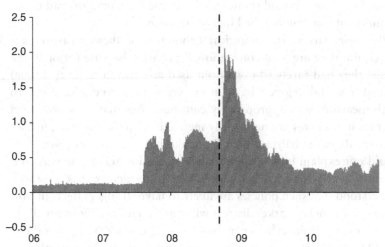

Figure 1.2 Three-month EURIBOR minus three-month OIS spread, in percentage points. Money market spreads fall following the introduction of ECB non-standard measures.
Source: Reuters

In previous work (Lenza et al. 2010), we argued that at a two-year horizon such measures supported credit growth by about 1.5 percentage points (in annualised terms) in the euro area, while reducing the rise in unemployment by about 0.5 percentage points. While clearly insufficient to arrest the downturn in economic activity in the euro area post-Lehman, the non-standard measures introduced by the ECB to support market functioning had an economically and statistically significant supportive effect on both the economy as a whole and on the stability of the financial sector.

1.2.2 Substituting for Standard Policy by Exploiting Unconventional Transmission Channels

Another set of non-standard policy measures aims at exploiting additional unconventional channels of monetary policy transmission, beyond the conventional impact of lower interest rates. Such measures are thus a potential *substitute* for conventional monetary policy, should the lower bound on nominal interest rates bind or traditional channels of transmission be blocked (or both).

By their nature, the empirical properties of these measures are uncertain: they are 'non-conventional' precisely because (prior to the crisis) they had rarely (if ever) been used and therefore (in real time) lacked a well-developed basis in empirical experience. Recourse to such measures was appropriately cautious.[6] But that does not mean that such measures are necessarily ineffective; on the contrary, former Federal Reserve chairman Ben Bernanke has argued that, even if he could not explain how such measures worked in theory, he was confident that they had worked in practice. In particular, it is now well understood that such policies are likely to have stronger effects in situations of financial market distress when arbitrage conditions are likely to fail and portfolio effects may be stronger (see Cardia and Woodford [2011] for a discussion of conditions under which the neutrality of these policies fail) and in general may have a justification if we think financial frictions are pervasive. Yet non-standard policy actions may come with side effects, and if in normal times their effect is likely to be

[6] For a discussion of the incentives for caution, see Orphanides and Wieland (2000), who develop the arguments of Brainard (1967) in this context.

small, the negative effect that they have on financial stability may be larger than the positive one on aggregate demand.

In the euro area, the leading example of such measures is the ECB's asset purchase programme introduced in mid-2014 and extended to sovereign debt in March 2015. On the basis of the ECB's own rhetoric, ECB asset purchases are intended to trigger portfolio balance effects. By buying sovereign debt and lowering the rate at which they remunerate excess reserves, central banks reduce the supply of and lower the return on 'safe' assets such as cash and government bonds. In response, the private sector – in order to maintain returns and sustain earnings – has to shift from safe to riskier assets, moving further out along the credit and maturity spectra in a 'search for yield'. The resulting strengthening of asset prices and expansion of credit creation will support activity and ultimately underpin price dynamics.

1.3 Potential Implications for Financial Stability

The nature of the non-standard measure determines its likely implications for financial stability.

1.3.1 'Passive' Unconventional Policies Tend to Support Financial Stability

At a time when private markets are 'seizing up' owing to concerns about counterparty credit risk, central bank intermediation can substitute for transactions that were previously undertaken between private parties, but which are hampered by market malfunctioning.

When expanding central bank intermediation, the ECB's role – and, in particular, the expansion of its balance sheet – is 'passive'. Banks make recourse to the ECB's facilities in the face of their own problems in undertaking transactions with each other. The increase in private risk-taking following the provision of central bank support represents a recovery from the defensive posture that underlay the malfunctioning of markets (e.g., reflected in hoarding of central bank liquidity and/or reluctance to assume private interbank counterparty credit risk). ECB interventions can be characterised as 'circuit breakers' halting a potentially vicious downward spiral of market dislocation and loss of market participants' confidence.

In essence, this is little more than a re-statement of Bagehot's (1873) rule. At times when liquidity in private interbank markets dries up, central banks should stand ready to 'lend freely to banks, but only against good collateral and at a penalty rate' so as to contain panic and prevent the breakdown of financial intermediation. Such action prevents contagion from one market segment to others and ultimately into the wider economy.

Expanding central bank intermediation to substitute for malfunctioning private markets should largely be supportive of financial stability (at least on impact). It is a defensive policy aimed at preventing a potentially catastrophic collapse of the broader financial system. The greater private risk-taking prompted by such central bank intermediation is an indication that the underpinning of the financial sector is working and private risk sentiment is returning to 'normal' pre-crisis levels.

1.3.2 'Active' Unconventional Policies May Threaten Financial Stability

By contrast, when seeking to prompt portfolio shifts, the ECB plays an 'active' role in the expansion of its balance sheet. The ECB itself initiates asset purchases and drives the pace and nature of the balance sheet expansion by its own choices. Rather than providing a backstop that helps private-sector risk-taking to recover towards more 'normal' levels, it is inherent in the portfolio balance transmission channel for ECB asset purchases that the central bank pushes asset managers into securities with risk profiles they would otherwise be sceptical about at prices they would otherwise deem too high.

This is the same effect that the central bank achieves through conventional easing via a decrease of the interest rate target: the central bank increases the incentive for the private sector to invest in riskier assets. Prompting private portfolio shifts into riskier assets may entail some risks to financial stability, but these may take different forms. Although both policies encourage risk intermediation, conventional policies encourage also maturity transformation whereas asset purchases do not (this observation has been recently formalized by Woodford [2016]).

The key difference is that while a decrease in the policy rate causes a decline in the equilibrium rate on riskier assets through an increase in the spreads, active balance sheet policies at the zero lower bound, by lowering the risk premium, have a dampening effect on the spread.

Yet, current financial stability concerns have emphasised the risks arising from a flat yield curve generated by the ECB quantitative policy, rather than its risk mitigation effects. Such a policy, it is argued, makes safe assets expensive and therefore encourages private investors into purchasing riskier instruments, prompting the squeezing of term premia and credit spreads that will ease general financial conditions, and, although this supports the economy, it also creates risks.

To the extent that banks earn returns from maturity transformation (as is the case for important segments of the European banking sector, particularly for the mutual and regional banks), the flatter yield curve implied by quantitative easing threatens their earnings outlook. For banks holding legacy portfolios of questionable assets and seeking to re-capitalise by retaining earnings, a flatter yield curve lengthens the period of adjustment (and may even make it infeasible). Moreover, for pension funds and insurance companies that have defined-benefit liabilities (i.e., they have promised a certain positive return to their customers), holding assets with low or negative returns (Figure 1.3) eats into their capital and reserves. Institutions that were poorly capitalised at the outset are, by nature, particularly vulnerable to these concerns.

The appendix provides a stylized summary table of the implications for financial stability of conventional and unconventional monetary policy easing.

1.3.3 Specific Measures May Have Both Passive and Active Elements

Let us go back to the distinction between 'active' and 'passive' central banks' balance sheet policies. The preceding discussion portrays a black-and-white distinction between these two different types. But in reality the distinction is rarely clear-cut. Many of the measures implemented by central banks during the financial crisis have elements which support market functioning as well as those that promote portfolio shifts and/or support macroeconomic stimulus.

For example, our characterisation of the ECB's fixed rate/full allotment operations as a 'passive' policy intervention providing a 'central

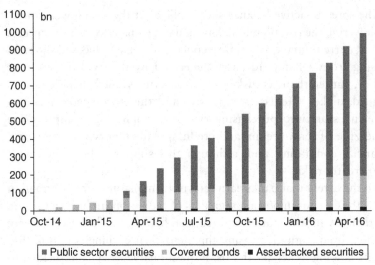

Figure 1.3 ECB asset purchases (in EUR bn.).
Source: ECB

counterpart of last resort' stems from the assumption that the ECB simply employed its own balance sheet to match banks long on liquidity
with banks short of liquidity, so as to clear the market. Since these transactions were collateralised, in principle the ECB took no credit risk, but
merely provided liquidity to a system that had seized up.

Given its access to the 'printing press' and consequent ability to create
liquidity at no cost in potentially unlimited amounts, a central bank is
uniquely well placed to provide this service. Doing so is an implication
of the Friedman (1969) rule: the central bank should satiate the private
demand for liquidity at the market interest rate.

In practice, central banks face a more complex challenge. As the events
of 2007–2008 amply demonstrate, making an assessment of bank credit
risk and/or the quality of the collateral offered at monetary policy operations is difficult. The Bagehot and Friedman rules assume liquidity problems can easily and immediately be distinguished from solvency or credit
problems in real time. That is never the case.

The ECB's fixed rate/full allotment operations therefore may be better characterised as the provision of a 'market maker of last resort'
rather than a central counterparty of last resort. The ECB took a position in the market, accepting risk on its balance sheet in the form of

transactions with banks of potentially uncertain creditworthiness and/ or accepting collateral of uncertain value.[7]

Taking such a position extends the role of the central bank beyond that of the mere liquidity provider envisaged by Walter Bagehot and Milton Friedman. Central banks are forced to take a view on the 'fair value' of an asset it accepts as collateral and/or a loan it makes to a risky bank. This entails making an assessment of whether (and how) market failure drives asset prices away from fair value and thus whether the risk implied by acting as a market maker of last resort is acceptable.

But crucially the actions of the central bank also influence the nature of the market failure. While individual banks concerned about idio-syncratic credit risk in their private counterparts are susceptible to a market failure owing to adverse selection,[8] the central bank is able to internalise the externalities caused by the resulting drying up of market liquidity by acting to sustain market functioning and thus change the nature of the idiosyncratic risk.

1.3.4 *General Equilibrium Implications Need to Be Kept in Mind before Coming to an Overall View*

The preceding sub-section brings out the potential macroeconomic consequence of unconventional central bank policy, which can extend beyond solving microeconomic problems at the level of individual institutions. More broadly, in coming to an overall assessment of non-standard policy actions, their general equilibrium implications – the effects of policies on the wider economy beyond their immediate impact on the financial sector, and the feedback into the financial system from those macroeconomic effects – also need to be taken into account.

We do not intend to be alarmist about the potential for financial stability to be impaired by the ECB's adoption of asset purchases (and other more proactive forms of central bank balance sheet expansion). After all, the ultimate objective of these policies is to revive aggregate

---

[7] Although the ECB in principle valued collateral at market prices, its ability to do so was compromised for those assets where markets seized up at the outset of the financial crisis, notably the market for asset-backed securities.

[8] This is the situation analysed by Heider et al. (2015).

demand and boost nominal growth. If successful, the beneficial effects of the improvement in macroeconomic conditions on financial stability would more than outweigh the short-run and partial implications discussed above. In response to criticism that its policies have weakened the financial sector, the ECB has repeatedly argued along these lines. By staving off the break-up of the euro area and supporting recovery, the ECB rightly believes it has more than compensated for the initial adverse impact of some of its unconventional policies on bank profitability.

Nor do we wish to downplay the potential negative effects of central bank intermediation. Re-establishing normal market functioning ultimately relies on normalising the behaviour of market participants. The central bank can support this process, but in the end it is the private sector that creates and maintains the market. Central banks must ensure that their support of the functioning of the financial sector during a crisis does not morph into a dependence of the financial sector on that support even in normal times.

By implication, necessary emergency measures should not blunt the incentives for governments, regulators and the private sector to address the underlying structural problems in the financial system and the economy more broadly. Should those incentives to deal with the fundamental weaknesses be absent, central bank intermediation could increase the risk to financial stability over the medium term. However this need not happen if the right policy mix is pursued.

The relationship between non-standard monetary policy measures and central bank balance sheet expansion, on the one hand, and the outlook for financial stability, on the other, is thus complex. While it depends crucially only on the character of the non-standard policy, it will also be influenced by other policy actions and the horizon over which an assessment is made.

In the context of the euro area, a key area of policy action is the consolidation of the banking sector, a solution for the stock of non-performing loans and a realistic approach for banks recapitalization. In a fragmented banking sector, with many banks still under-capitalized, potential risks to financial stability stemming from non-standard measures are real and potentially significant but these problems can be addressed with different policy tools.

1.4 The Implications of Some Recent Empirical Results

A number of recent empirical analyses of euro area data shed light on the issues described earlier, showing how non-standard monetary policy measures can influence financial stability in a variety of ways.

Koijen et al. (2016) explore a unique data set on the securities holdings by different categories of investors across euro area countries. They investigate how ECB asset purchases have influenced the sectoral holdings of these securities over time and the distribution of risk among the central bank and various types of intermediaries. Their estimates show that in the three quarters since the beginning of the ECB extended asset purchase program (APP) in January 2015, the foreign sector and banks, whose response to the ECB purchases has been the most elastic, have seen a decline in their share of duration risk. The results reveal heterogeneity among financial institutions' reaction to APP and, in particular, a different behaviour between banks and institutional investors. Facing a risk–return tradeoff, institutions' reaction is driven by both hedging and speculative motives. The former leads to inelasticity in response to APP and prevails among pension funds and insurance companies, whereas the latter motivates elasticity and prevails in banks.

The different behaviour of banks and institutional investors can be rationalised as follows. In line with the argumentation offered in Andrade et al. (2016), banks that are holding large portfolios of domestic (peripheral) sovereign debt stand to make large capital gains as central bank purchases of government bonds reduce the sovereign spread of peripheral over core countries. The resulting strengthening of the banks' capital position serves to support the stability of both individual banks and the banking system as a whole.

In this context, banks are prepared to sell bonds into the asset purchase programme, so as to realise those capital gains and increase their balance sheet flexibility. In principle, that new flexibility could be used to extend additional bank credit to the private sector – one example of the shift into riskier and less liquid assets that the 'portfolio balance' channel of transmission of central bank asset purchases is intended to generate. In practice – in the face of a still weak demand for credit in the euro area and the additional regulatory capital requirements imposed on banks – the balance sheet flexibility has largely been used to support a more orderly deleveraging. All of this is broadly supportive of financial stability.

Yet this capital gain enjoyed by the banks is a one-off benefit of the asset purchase programme. Once sovereign spreads have shrunk and the risk-free yield curve has been flattened through the squeezing of sovereign credit risk and term premia by central bank asset purchases, banks face a flat and (in a context of negative policy rates) low yield structure. For banks reliant on short-term funding and extracting returns from maturity transformation, this is a difficult environment.

Indeed Hazell and Pill (2016) show that further central bank easing from this point can weigh on the outlook for bank earnings. Using changes in the five-year swap rate around ECB press conferences as a proxy for monetary easing on both conventional and unconventional dimensions (on the basis that this will capture not only changes in policy rates, but also the impact of forward guidance and asset purchases), they find that such innovations weigh on bank equity performance relative to a broad euro area equity index. They thus conclude that even if the start of asset purchases yielded a one-off capital gain for banks, the impact of further non-standard policies from here on bank earnings is viewed (at least by equity market participants) as negative after that initial effect. Looking forward, threats to the earnings potential and thus stability of the financial sector could emerge, as additional non-standard measures are implemented. Such concerns are at the heart of recent policy debates in both Europe and Japan. As we commented earlier, the significance of this argument must be evaluated on the basis of a broader quantitative assessment of the macroeconomic effect and distribution of risk effects of the policy in discussion.

Relative to banks, life assurance and pension funds enjoy less balance sheet flexibility. The nature of their business (in conjunction with the current regulatory regime) forces them to hold long-duration assets to match their long-duration liabilities. Although they also have made significant capital gains on their holdings of government debt as a consequence of central bank asset purchases, they face the problem of having to reinvest in long-duration assets that now offer very low returns.

To the extent that pension funds have defined benefit liabilities that promise positive nominal returns, the emergence of very low or even negative yields on long-dated sovereign debt poses a threat to their business model if it persists. In that context, seeking to 'ride out' the low-yield environment by holding onto the existing debt paying higher coupons and waiting for a revival of yields before reinvesting makes sense. But should that revival of yields not happen, the viability of the institutional pension business model is in question, raising significant financial stability risks.

In short, the (albeit still limited) empirical evidence available on the response of financial institutions to Eurosystem non-standard policy measures is consistent with the view that banks and asset managers stand to benefit from the impact of ECB asset purchases in the short term, but will suffer if the low and flat yield curve environment created by unconventional policy persists for some time. By implication, non-standard measures can support financial stability in the short run, but should those measures not produce the desired macroeconomic revival of growth and inflation expectations to re-steepen the yield curve, financial stability may be at risk at longer horizons.

1.5 More Emphasis on the Appropriate Macrofinancial Policy Mix

In the preceding sections, we described how the squeeze on financial institutions' earnings associated with negative policy rates and sovereign debt purchases may create and perpetuate financial stability risks, especially in an environment where banks, insurers and pension funds are already poorly capitalised as a consequence of the financial crisis.

Yet such a squeeze on financials' earnings is a key link in the transmission of the ECB's asset purchase programme. To induce the desired 'search for yield' in riskier and longer duration assets, central bank actions must have an effect on private investors' earnings, so as to induce the shift out of safe assets.

Where the preferred habitat for safe assets is strong – as is the case for many German banks and asset managers, for a mixture of cultural and regulatory reasons – the pressure required to induce such a shift is greater. In particular, following the sovereign and banking crises of 2011–2012, many German institutions have been reluctant to hold peripheral assets at any price (or return) (Figure 1.4). The reputational risk of potentially taking losses on non-core sovereign or private instruments is deemed too great.

In short, flattening the German sovereign yield curve to weigh on the earnings of German financial institutions is a necessary part of the transmission process of unconventional policies such as quantitative

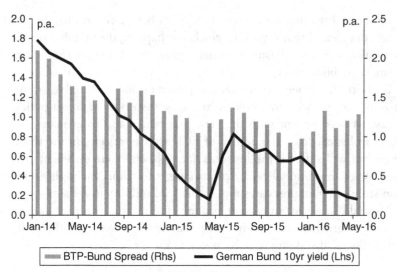

Figure 1.4 German sovereign yields and spreads against Italian sovereign debt. Percent per annum (LHS), percentage points (RHS).
Source: ECB

easing (QE). If German institutions remain reluctant to shift into riskier peripheral or corporate instruments despite the yield differentials that QE has opened up, the logic of unconventional policy measures implies that greater pressure – in other words, more QE and further flattening of the yield curve – is needed. No pain, no gain.

The challenge facing euro area policymakers is to ensure that the pressure to engage in portfolio rebalancing into riskier and longer maturity assets is maintained, without endangering financial institutions' profitability to the extent that a process that endangers financial stability is triggered. Moreover, they must be confident that the macroeconomic impact of non-standard policy measures on growth and inflation expectations comes through to steepen and raise the yield curve, so as to revive the earnings potential of banks and institutional investors, before the financial sector faces a crisis of its existing business model and idiosyncratic and systemic financial stability risks build.

Such considerations have already achieved prominence in Scandinavia and the United Kingdom, prompting more discussion about the appropriate 'macrofinancial policy mix' across (both conventional and unconventional) monetary policy, macroprudential policies and microprudential supervision and regulation, as well as fiscal policy.

This is a debate that is set to become more important in the euro area, where the cross-country dimension promises to add further spice. With a new institutional environment emerging in the context of banking and capital markets union and macroprudential measures as yet untested, maintaining the appropriate balance across policies will be a difficult challenge.

Some have proposed that additional pressure is applied for financial institutions to diversify across holdings of euro area sovereign and private assets (Garicano and Reichlin, 2014 a,b; Brunnemeier et al. 2016; Corsetti et al. 2016). For example, only allowing a zero risk weighting for diversified portfolios of government debt on bank balance sheets would force a shift into peripheral debt by core banks (and vice versa), without requiring the earnings squeeze associated with a very flat and low core sovereign yield curve.

But the political and practical problems associated with such mechanisms are obvious (as responses to the proposal illustrate): using an administrative approach to overcome the strong home bias of German institutions' asset holdings is unlikely to be well received by the institutions themselves, while the shedding of peripheral debt by peripheral institutions raises questions about the transition. These considerations give a flavour of the difficult trade-offs in developing an appropriate macrofinancial policy mix in the euro area.

References

Andrade, P., J. Breckenfelder, F. De Fiore, P. Karadi and O. Tristani (2016). The ECB's asset purchase programme: An early assessment. ECB Working Paper No. 1956. Frankfurt: European Central Bank.

Bagehot, W. (1873). *Lombard Street: A description of the money market.* London: H.S. King & Co.

Brainard, W. (1967). Uncertainty and the effectiveness of policy. *American Economic Review* 57(2), 411–425.

Brunnemeier, M., S. Langfield, M. Pagano, R. Reis, S. Van Nieuwerburgh, R. Reis, S. Van Nieuwerburghk and D. Vayanos (2016). ESBies: Safety is in the tranches. Working paper from 2016, CFS Working Paper Series, No. 537.

Cardia, V. and M. Woodford (2011). The central bank balance sheet as an instrument of monetary policy. *Journal of Monetary Economics* 58 (1), 54–79.

Corsetti, G. C., L. Feld, L. Reichlin, R. Reis, H. Rey and B. Weder di Mauro. (2016). Reinforcing the Eurozone and protecting an open society. Washington, DC: Center for Economic and Policy Research.

Friedman, M. (1969). The Demand for Money-Some Theoretical and Empirical Results. In The Optimum Quantity of Money and Other Essays. Chicago: Aldine, 1969.

Garicano, L. and L. Reichlin (2014a). Squaring the Eurozone's vicious circle. *Project Syndicate*, 27 January.

(2014b). A safe asset for the Eurozone: A proposal. *Vox-EU: CEPR's Policy Portal*, 14 November.

Giannone, D., M. Lenza, H. Pill and L.Reichlin (2012). The ECB and the interbank market. *Economic Journal* 122, 467–486.

Hazell, J. and H. Pill (2016). Monetary policy transmission: When rates are (very) low, the bank lending channel is weak. *European Economics Analyst*, 15 September.

Heider, F., M. Hoerova and C. Holthausen (2015). Liquidity hoarding and interbank market spreads: The role of counterparty risk. *Journal of Financial Economics* 118(2), 336–354.

Koijen, R.S.J., F. Koulischer, B. Nguyen and M. Yogo (2016). Quantitative easing in the euro area: The dynamics of risk exposures and the impact on asset prices. Banque de France document de travail no. 601.

Lenza, M., H. Pill and L. Reichlin (2010). Monetary policy in exceptional times. *Economic Policy* 62, 295–339.

Meltzer, A. (2009). Inflation nation. *New York Times*, 3 May.

Orphanides, A. and V. Wieland (2000). Efficient monetary policy design near price stability. *Journal of the Japanese and International Economies* 14(4), 327–265.

Pill, H. (2010). Monetary policy in a low interest rate environment: A checklist. *International Seminar on Macroeconomics* 6, 335–345.

Reichlin, L. and S. Valle (2016). Resolving the banking crisis in Italy. *Project Syndicate*, 14 October 2016.

Weidmann, J. (2016). A look at the euro area from a central bank perspective. Keynote speech to the Second Lichtenstein Financial Forum, 23 March.

Woodford, M. (2016). Quantitative easing and financial stability. NBER Working Paper 22285. Cambridge, MA: National Bureau of Economic Research.

Appendix: Stylized Summary of the Effect of Conventional Monetary Policy Easing and 'Active' Asset Purchases

	Direct impact	Implications for financial stability
Conventional monetary policy (easing)	Lowers whole yield curve, reducing breakeven on capital projects, etc.	+ Via impact on economic growth[a] – via possible promotion of asset price bubbles[a]
	Steepens yield curve, increasing incentive for maturity transformation	– Via impact on banks' vulnerability
Unconventional policy: asset purchases	Lowers whole yield curve, reducing breakeven on capital projects, etc.	+ Via impact on economic growth[a] – Via possible promotion of asset price bubbles[a]
	Flattens yield curve, reducing incentive for maturity transformation	+ Via impact on banks' vulnerability – Via impact on banks + insurance companies' profitability
Unconventional policy: market maker of last resort	Restores banks access to short term funding	+ Via impact on banks' funding + Via encouragement of credit flows, hence impact on economic activity, etc.

[a]All these consequences – good and bad – were prompted by the 'search for yield'.

2 | Financial Innovation and Financial Stability: An Introduction

SEPPO HONKAPOHJA

2.1 Introduction: The Global Financial Crisis and the Crisis in Europe

The start of the global financial crisis can be dated in different ways. One plausible date is August 9, 2007, when significant turmoil in financial markets appeared after activity closures in some hedge funds specializing in US mortgage debt were announced.

The scale and the economic ramifications of the crisis have been vast (see Figure 2.1). The resulting economic downturn in 2008 for awhile resembled the pace of developments during the Great Depression (see, e.g. Rajan 2013). Liquidity support operations by central banks at different stages, explicit state guarantees to banks and expansionary fiscal policies succeeded in stopping the recession and changed the course of developments in comparison to the 1930s.

In Europe, a further stage of the crisis appeared in 2010 when a sovereign debt crisis hit some euro area countries. It has been suggested that the euro crisis has its roots in the specific features of construction of the European Monetary Union but also that it was triggered by the second-wave shocks following the global financial crisis.

The financial crisis weakened the euro area economies and it also weakened bank balance sheets. In several countries governments were forced to support their troubled banks, which in turn adversely affected government finances. In some countries public finances became weak, which fed back to the credibility of their banking sectors, thus creating a notorious bank–sovereign feedback loop.

Troubled countries' membership in the monetary union added to the challenge to restore their competitiveness, as traditional tools such as devaluation were no longer available. It became evident that the fiscal rules agreed on in the monetary union had not always been

I am grateful for Esa Jokivuolle, Hanna Westman and Aleksi Vänttinen for assistance and comments.

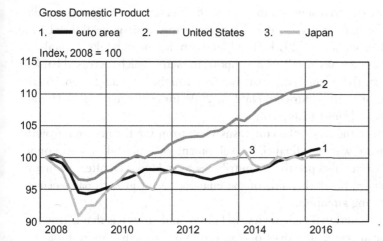

Sources: National statistical authorities, Eurostat and Macrobond.

Figure 2.1 Gross domestic product (GDP).
Sources: National Statistical authorities, Eurostat and Macrobond

honored. These developments raised concerns about credibility of the weak euro area countries in international capital markets. The so-called existential risk of the euro zone emerged.

The culmination of the eurocrisis in mid-2012 was tamed by the creation of the European Central Bank (ECB)'s outright monetary transactions (OMT) program. I quote President Draghi's promise that "Within [its] mandate, the ECB is ready to do whatever it takes to preserve the euro."[1] OMT is a conditional promise to buy in the secondary market without limit government bonds of selected euro area countries. OMT has worked, and, remarkably, there has so far not been any need to activate the program.

2.2 Finance and Economic Growth

Thinking with hindsight about the causes and possible early indicators of the financial crises, one thing seems clear. The financial sector, including banks, grew to a very large scale in many countries.

---

[1] Speech by Mario Draghi, president of the European Central Bank at the Global Investment Conference in London 26 July 2012. Further details of OMT were subsequently specified by the Governing Council of the ECB.

Recent research suggests that when the financial sector grows rapidly into large proportions, the risk of a serious crisis is heightened (see e.g. Claessens et al. 2014). The long-term decline in banks' capital-to-assets ratios has also been an important factor which increased banks' fragility (referring to the past, as a factor in the preceding financial crisis, see e.g. Alessandri and Haldane 2009 for evidence from the United States and United Kingdom).

Before the crisis, the consensus view from the finance and growth literature was that financial development not only follows economic growth but also positively contributes to it. However, after the financial crisis, the darker side of the financial sector growth has received increasing attention.

The traditional benign view of finance and growth is that a growing financial sector improves overall economic growth opportunities by mobilizing resources to finance investment projects and by facilitating risk management. The key assumption is that a well-developed financial system helps allocate productive resources more efficiently, both by channeling funds to growth sectors and by pulling resources from declining ones.

Correspondingly, research has argued that low financial development could be a factor which reduces long-run growth and also increases growth volatility (see e.g. Aghion, Farhi and Kharroubi 2012 and the literature cited therein). However, recent research suggests that while finance does contribute to economic growth, it does so only up to a point (see e.g. Cecchetti and Kharroubi 2012).

At the level of individual financial institutions, the growth of bank balance sheets was seen as reflecting increasing returns to scale and scope from combining a wide variety of financial services and providing them also cross-border to internationally active clients.

Technological development and financial innovation enabled the creation of totally new products. These were initially seen as filling gaps in the palette of risk management products and creating totally new segments of the financial markets (see Rajan 2005 and also Bolton 2016).

Today we know that many of the new exciting risk management products increase rather than reduce risk, when applied inappropriately. Moreover, the changing shape of financial intermediation and risk management made the whole financial system more vulnerable to common shocks.

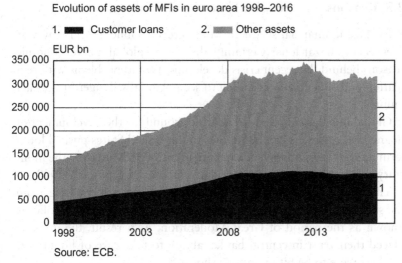

Figure 2.2 Evolution of assets of MFIs in euro area, 1998–2016.
Source: ECB

In the crisis the ultimate risk stemmed largely from the US housing market, but it had been transferred also onto European banks' balance sheets (Shin 2012). This took place with the help of securitizations and the related new financial intermediaries, generally dubbed as the shadow banking sector. As a result, the number of counterparty relationships and the ensuing counterparty risks increased. The global financial network became highly interconnected and complex, reducing transparency, which eventually resulted in a dramatic evaporation of trust. Figure 2.2 reflects these developments in the euro area: banks' total assets grew both in absolute terms and as a share of GDP, and much of the growth took place in assets other than customer loans.

Many of these developments prior to the crisis may not have benefitted the real economy in a sustainable manner. Economic recovery from the crisis has been slow (see e.g. Claessens et al. 2014).

One important lesson from the crisis is the need to understand better the point where and why the expansion of the financial sector, or any of its particular business areas, turns excessive. Moreover, we need to ensure that financial innovations such as securitization are applied appropriately so that the benefits are realized.

2.3 Reasons for Excessive Financial Growth

Why did the financial sector this time grow so much? And why was it especially hazardous? Certainly, there were global macroeconomic reasons behind the recent crisis developments, and problems with regulation and supervision in failing to see potentially dangerous market failures.

Global imbalances provided a fertile ground for the development of financial excesses, as capital inflows to the United States pushed long-term interest rates down (see e.g. Bernanke 2005). Moreover, the monetary policy stance was accommodative in much of the early 2000s.

There may also have been a false sense of security resulting from the successful track record of monetary and macroeconomic policies, known as the period of Great Moderation. As a result, the markets placed their trust in central banks' ability to take care of liquidity if markets were to be hit by serious shocks.

These expectations may also have contributed to imprudent risk-taking which, once the crisis started unfolding, led to real losses. Banks' capital requirements and liquidity buffers had not kept pace with the growing risks as serious shortcomings in risk measurement and lack of loss-absorbing capital within the Basel framework became apparent once the crisis hit.

Theoretical models of the possibility of excessive financial growth range from banks' failure to internalize systemic risks from growth of bank leverage and ballooning balance sheets to rent-extraction in opaque over-the-counter (OTC) markets (see e.g. Stein 2012 and Bolton, Santos and Scheinkman 2012, respectively). Research has also shown how financial innovation waves can raise the risk of an endogenous crisis (see Biais, Rochet and Woolley 2010). Moreover, as financial innovation caters to investors' desire for safe assets, systemic risk may follow if these new "safe" assets turn out to be highly risky, as happened in the last crisis (see Gennaioli, Shleifer and Vishny 2012).

Cross-country evidence indicates that financial innovation does contribute to economic growth, especially in industries dependent on external finance. In light of the recent crisis, such innovation also contributes to growth volatility, idiosyncratic bank risk and bank losses (Beck, Chen and Song 2012).

Compensation schemes focusing on short-term performance became popular in the last decade and they were said to encourage risk-taking in new financial products which generated fee income (see e.g. Rajan 2005).

Market expectations of public support in the event of a large-scale crisis may well have been an important reason for excessive financial growth. For instance, the leading European banks are very large in an international comparison, especially in relation to the size of their home countries (see Liikanen 2012).

Many large and complex financial institutions appear to have benefited from cheap funding, thanks to such too-big-to-fail expectations (see e.g. Davies and Tracey 2014). Cheap funding which is insensitive to balance sheet risks may easily spur risk-taking, especially when banking competition gets tougher. Sheer ignorance by bank managements of the true risks may also have played a role (Rajan 2013). Some have argued that deregulation around 2000 in the United States, such as the repeal of the Glass–Steagall Act, was the reason why contractual risk-taking incentives were raised especially in the biggest banks, perhaps in order to spur banks to pursue the new growth opportunities in the deregulated business environment (cf. e.g. DeYoung, Peng and Yan 2013). More research on the effects of deregulation would still be welcome to further clarify these questions.

The too-big-to-fail phenomenon weakened market discipline, and the opacity of large complex financial institutions contributed to this. The structure of the banking sector has not been reformed in a way that accords with well-established market discipline (cf. Laeven and Levine 2007). The challenge is to implement regulatory reforms and policies that steer the financial sector and banks towards a size and structure that best support economic growth. At the same time financial stability should be maintained.

No one really knows the right size of the financial sector or banks. For instance, it has been pointed out that the scale and scope of the largest banks may simply be an efficient response by banks to the bundles of services demanded by the big, internationally active customers (see Bolton 2016). At least, attempt should be made to remove any perverse incentives which can lead to excessive growth of the sector and its risks. Eliminating the too-big-to-fail problem lies at the core of the solution.

2.4 Financial Reforms after the Crises

A profound international regulatory reform agenda was endorsed by the G-20 in response to the global financial crisis. Many key parts of the agenda, especially the Basel III framework, have been implemented.

The European Union has launched its own additional financial reform program, called the banking union, in response to the euro crisis. The banking union entails a common banking supervision and a framework for bank resolution. The Single Supervisory Mechanism is operated by the ECB and has been in place since November 2014. The establishment of the Single Resolution Mechanism in the European Union facilitates the resolution of cross-border banks.[2]

Importantly, the resolution framework removes bail-out, subject to certain exceptions, from the crisis management toolkit. The framework gives the power to authorities to implement a "bail-in" of bank debt holders, provided the bail-in is in the public interest. Bail-in means that debt holders will bear losses without actual bankruptcy proceedings.[3] Because bail-in is not a default event, it in principle reduces a bank's probability of default. On balance, however, the limitation on bail-outs would probably lead to higher expected losses to debt holders.

To make bail-in a credible resolution tool, banks will have to have a minimum amount of loss-absorbing capacity such as equity or bail-inable debt instruments. Loss-absorbing capacity should be sufficiently high so that a bank can be recapitalized after a failure to the extent that it can again obtain funding from the market.

The key motivation for the banking union is to break the notorious bank–sovereign feedback loop, match the institutional structure (supervisor and resolution authority) with the geographic scope of the cross-border banks and pave the way for further banking integration. True banking integration in Europe could also enhance financial stability in the European Union by reversing the fragmentation of financial conditions in the aftermath of the crisis, which is apparently hampering Europe's current economic recovery.

However, some recent experiences have also raised questions about the functionality of the bail-in framework. One concern is that potential

---

[2] For a detailed review of the post-crisis regulatory reforms in the United States, with some comparison with the European reforms, see Chapter 3.

[3] An important precondition is that debt holders' losses have to be less than they would be in bankruptcy proceedings.

investors in debt instruments, which are subject to bail-in, are really provided with realistic information of the true risks involved. The responsibility lies with the banks, but the processes related to investor protection are closely monitored by the supervisor.

Another concern is contagion, of which the volatile price behavior of banks' contingent convertible (CoCo) bonds in early 2016 was a reminder. CoCos are contingent convertible bonds that can automatically convert to equity when the issuing banks' financial position weakens. The key reform which supports the bail-in framework by mitigating contagion is that banks' equity base has improved as a result of higher minimum requirements. Moreover, limits on holdings of other banks' bail-inable debt will further reduce the contagion risk.

The banking union project also includes a third element: the prospect of creating a common deposit insurance system. However, the national systems currently vary a great deal, so that the first priority is harmonization of the national systems of deposit insurance.

There are also a number of other regulatory initiatives in addition to the banking union. Some initiatives focus on increased transparency in the financial markets. For example, accounting standards and disclosure practices are reviewed, and banks are urged to improve risk management and corporate governance practices. Other initiatives including supervision and regulation of derivatives markets and the shadow banking system are revised, including moves to central counterparties which will help address the contagion risks embedded in long counterparty chains in the OTC markets.

An obvious question is whether the increased regulation of banking will lead to the growth of the less regulated shadow banking sector. Would systemic risks also migrate from banking to shadow banking as a result of the new banking regulation? There are responses to this concern that aim to increase transparency and oversight of shadow banking.[4] Some researchers have also suggested that regulatory margin requirements, an equivalent of banks' capital requirements, could be considered for shadow banking institutions (see Hanson, Kashyap and Stein 2010). This would reduce the risk of fire sales and the resulting loss spirals which were experienced during the global financial crisis both in banks and shadow banks. It is also crucial to make sure

---

[4] For example, the rules enhancing the transparency of securities financing transactions were enacted in October 2015 (see European Commission 2015).

that banks' exposures to shadow banks are met with sufficient capital requirements.

Macroprudential analysis and tools are another area of regulation that has truly emerged only after the crisis. They are being developed mainly on the national basis, but also in accordance with Basel III and the capital requirement directive (its application in Europe) for the purpose of setting counter-cyclical capital buffers. Moreover, the European Systemic Risk Board has published guidelines on the implementation of macroprudential tools across the EU member states. This is a highly important but challenging area of work where we are most likely to see a lot more research and new developments in the future. The challenge is to find indicators which are able to warn of looming vulnerabilities sufficiently early. Potential candidates are at least market prices, credit-to-GDP ratios, and changes in banking sector liabilities (see e.g. Shin 2014).

Finally, in accordance with the structural regulation of banks already agreed in the United States and the United Kingdom, the European Commission has proposed a ban on proprietary trading for the largest banks and an option for subsidiarization of other trading activities, to be placed in a separate legal entity within a banking group. The motivation for the structural regulation is to significantly reduce, together with the resolution framework, the largest banks' too-big-to-fail status.

2.5 Conclusions

I conclude by discussing some open issues in modelling financial instability and its real economic consequences in order to guide future policies. It seems that macro models in which crises arise endogenously with long-lasting effects on medium-term economic growth may not yet be well suited to simulate the effects of various macroprudential policy instruments which policymakers need to assess before implementation. In contrast, more detailed macro models which can incorporate various macroprudential policy simulations are mainly business cycle models with financial frictions but without actual crisis events. Hence they may provide only limited opportunities to do welfare analysis of macroprudential policies, given the empirical evidence of the substantial real economic costs of crises. This is currently a big challenge in macro research.

Further, we should also ask what the right balance between micro-prudential and macroprudential policies is. There has already been interesting work in this area, which suggests that in pursuing macroprudential aims sufficiently high minimum capital requirements, i.e. a standard microprudential policy tool, are more important than dynamically adjusting macroprudential capital buffers over time (see Mendicino et al. 2015). Because the level of bank capital is directly linked to the degree of banks' solvency and hence stability of the financial system, the research agenda on incorporating crises in sufficiently realistic macro models appears all the more important.

References

Aghion, P., E. Farhi and E. Kharroubi (2012). Monetary policy, liquidity, and growth. NBER Working Paper 18072. Cambridge, MA: National Bureau of Economic Research.

Alessandri, P. and A. G. Haldane (2009). Banking on the state. Bank of England, November 2009.

Beck, T., T. Chen, C. Lin and F.M. Song (2012). Financial innovation: The bright and the dark sides. HKIMR Working Paper 05/2012. Hong Kong: Hong Kong Institute for Monetary Research.

Bernanke, B. S. (2005). The global saving glut and the U.S. current account deficit. Speech delivered at the Sandridge Lecture, Virginia Association of Economists, Richmond, Virginia, March 10, 2005.

Biais, B., J-C. Rochet and P. Woolley (2010). Innovations, rents and risk. The Paul Woolley Centre Discussion Paper No. 659. London: The Paul Woolley Centre for the Sudy of Capital Market Dysfunctionality.

Bolton, P. (2016). The Good banker. In E. Glaeser, T. Santos and G. Weyl (eds.), *Après le Déluge: Finance and the Common Good after the Crisis*. Chicago: University of Chicago Press.

Bolton, P., T. Santos and J. Scheinkman (2012). Cream skimming in financial markets. NBER Working Paper 16804. Cambridge, MA: National Bureau of Economic Research.

Cecchetti, S. and E. Kharroubi (2012). Reassessing the impact of finance on growth. BIS Working Paper 381. Basel: Bank for International Settlements.

Claessens, S., M.A. Kose, L. Laeven and F. Valencia (eds.) (2014). *Understanding Financial Crises: Causes, Consequences, and Policy Responses*. Washington, DC: International Monetary Fund.

Davies, R. and B. Tracey (2014). Too big to be efficient? The impact of implicit funding subsidies on scale economies in banking. *Journal of Money, Credit and Banking* 46:1, 219–253.

DeYoung, R., Peng, E. Y. and Yan, M. (2013). Executive compensation and business policy choices at U.S. commercial banks. *Journal of Financial and Quantitative Analysis* 48, 165–196.

Draghi, M. (2012). Speech in London. Available at www.ecb.europa.eu/press/key/date/2012/html/sp120726.en.html.

European Commission (2015). European Parliament adopts Commission proposal to improve transparency of the shadow banking sector. Press release 29 October 2015.

Gennaioli, N., A. Shleifer and R.W. Vishny (2012). Neglected risks, financial innovation and financial fragility. *Journal of Financial Economics* 104:3, 452–468.

Hanson, S. G., A. K. Kashyap and J. C. Stein (2010). A macroprudential approach to financial regulation. *Journal of Economic Perspectives* 25:1, 3–28.

Laeven, L. and R. Levine (2007). Is there a diversification discount in financial conglomerates? *Journal of Financial Economics* 85:2, 331–367.

Liikanen, E. (2012). High-level Expert Group on reforming the structure of the EU banking sector (final report). Brussels.

Mendicino, C., K. Nikolov, J. Suarez and D. Supera (2015). Welfare analysis of implementable macroprudential policy rules: Heterogeneity and trade-offs. Available at www.cemfi.es/~suarez/MNSS_2015.pdf.

Rajan, R. (2005). Has finance made the world riskier? In *The Greenspan Era: Lessons for the Future*, Federal Reserve Bank of Kansas City. Also published in *European Financial Management*, 12:4, 2006, 499–533.

(2013). A step in the dark: Unconventional monetary policy after the crisis. Andrew Crockett Memorial Lecture, Bank for International Settlements, 23 June 2013.

Shin, H. S. (2012). Global banking glut and loan risk premium. *IMF Economic Review*, 60, 155–192.

(2014). Procyclicality and the search for early warning indicators. In Claessens, S., M. A. Kose, L. Laeven and F. Valencia (eds.), *Understanding Financial Crises: Causes, Consequences, and Policy Responses*, pp. 157–171. Washington, DC: International Monetary Fund.

Stein, J. (2012). Monetary policy as financial-stability regulation. *Quarterly Journal of Economics* 127, 57–95.

3 | Post-Crisis Changes in US Bank Prudential Regulation

LARRY D. WALL

3.1 Introduction

The leaders of the G-7 agreed in 2009 to take a variety of actions to reduce the risk of future financial crises.[1] Since then the United States has worked with other prudential supervisors in international bodies, such as the Basel Committee for Banking Supervision (BCBS), to strengthen banking regulation both to lower the risk of future crises and reduce the losses in the event of a crisis. However, the US efforts have not been limited to implementing international agreements. In many cases the United States went beyond the minimal requirements of the agreement, adopting stricter versions which are sometimes referred to as being "super equivalent." Additionally, the United States took a variety of measures that were unrelated to international agreements, albeit many of these measures had parallel action taken in other jurisdictions.

The US decision to make changes beyond those required by international agreements reflects several factors. First, the United States suffered trillions of dollars in lost output despite extraordinary financial intervention by the Federal Deposit Insurance Corporation, Federal Reserve, and US Treasury to stabilize the financial system.[2] In contrast, the financial systems of many developed (and developing) countries did not experience such a large shock to their financial systems. Second, the United States took prompt action to force recapitalization of its surviving banks and did not suffer a subsequent financial shock

[1] See G-7 (2009).
[2] See United States Government Accountability Office (2013).

The views expressed are those of the author and do not necessarily reflect those of the Federal Reserve Bank of Atlanta, the Federal Reserve System, or their staffs. The author thanks Esa Jokivuolle, Tom Noe, Hanna Westman and participants at the conference "From the Last Financial Crisis to the Next: Looking on the Horizon" for helpful comments on an earlier version of the chapter titled "Changes in the Expected Cost of Financial Instability: Some Developments since the Crisis."

38   *Larry D. Wall*

such as the European sovereign debt crisis. Thus, the US banks had some ability to move into compliance with tougher regulatory standards while continuing to supply credit to the real economy. Third, the United States has recognized too-big-to-fail (TBTF) banks as an important policy issue since the collapse of Continental Illinois in 1984 and took various policy measures to prevent TBTF in 1991.[3] The 2007–2009 crisis demonstrated that the earlier measures were inadequate. Congress attempted to remedy the observed deficiencies with its passage of the Dodd–Frank Wall Street Reform and Consumer Protection Act (DFA), which contains a number of provisions intended to make large banks less risky and to facilitate their resolution without taxpayer assistance if they do fail.

This chapter reviews the changes in prudential regulation of banking organizations adopted by the United States in the wake of the financial crisis with an emphasis on measures where the US changes went beyond internationally agreed reforms. The chapter is organized as follows. Sections 3.2 and 3.3 address the related issues of changes in capital adequacy regulation and accounting rules. Section 3.4 discusses new liquidity regulations. Section 3.5 discusses actions taken to prevent incentive compensation from creating undue risk taking incentives. Section 3.6 considers measures taken to reduce banks' exposure to financial market risk. Section 3.7 addresses issues related to bank size and complexity. The chapter concludes with a few summary remarks.

3.2 Capital Adequacy

At the start of the crisis, the international standard for bank capital was based on the Basel Committee on Banking Supervision (2004) agreement, widely referred to as Basel II. Basel II was intended to be more risk sensitive than Basel I.[4] Basel II gave banks a choice of adopting a standardized model with prespecified risk weights or the banks could choose one of two internal ratings based models (IRB),

[3] See Wall (2010) for a discussion of how the Federal Deposit Insurance Corporation Improvement Act in 1991 sought to end too-big-to-fail.
[4] The original Basel I was published as Basel Committee on Banking Supervision (1988). Note, each of the Basel capital accords has been modified several times after its respective adoption date as supervisors identify areas that need strengthening.

the foundation IRB and the advanced IRB. However, US commercial banking organizations had not yet adopted Basel II but were instead subject to the earlier Basel I risk-based capital requirements and a minimum leverage requirement. The US supervisors had taken the position that Basel II was mandatory only for internationally active banks and did not intend to apply it to smaller banks. The progress toward adoption of Basel II by the largest banks was slowed by quantitative impact studies that showed banks adopting Basel II may have been able to significantly reduce their holdings of regulatory capital.[5] This led the Federal Deposit Insurance Corporation (FDIC) and some members of Congress to express concern about the implications of the lower requirements for the capital adequacy of the adopters and for the competitive advantage this would give them relative to smaller banks.[6]

The BCBS agreed after the crisis that Basel II had not required banks to hold a sufficient amount of high-quality capital and adopted Basel Committee on Banking Supervision (2010), which is commonly referred to as Basel III. The US supervisors followed that agreement with a decision to require all US banks with assets greater than $500 million to comply with Basel III.[7]

One important change in Basel III is that it tightens the requirements for instruments to qualify as capital, especially the narrower measure of capital called Tier 1 capital. The goal of this change was to make sure that Tier 1 consisted of items that could absorb losses outside bankruptcy or resolution. Additionally, Basel III redefines the way some risks are measured, especially counterparty risk, to more adequately capture these risks.

Basel III also includes several changes that go beyond merely redefining capital and changing the way risk-weighted assets were calculated. One important change is the adoption of a minimum leverage ratio requirement (defined in this case as the ratio of capital to assets).[8] The

[5] See Board of Governors of the Federal Reserve System, Federal Deposit Insurance Corporation, Office of the Comptroller of the Currency, and Office of Thrift Supervision (2006).

[6] For example, see Bair (2007).

[7] The Federal Reserve Board maintains a page dedicated to the US implementation of the Basel accords at www.federalreserve.gov/bankinforeg/basel/USImplementation.htm

[8] The version of the leverage ratio adopted in Basel III includes exposures to off-balance sheet positions that had not been included in the pre-crisis version of the US leverage ratio.

leverage ratio requirement was added to the risk-based asset requirement to set a floor on the extent to which a bank could reduce its capital by overweighting exposure to assets that carried low risk-weights but which could prove risky in some circumstances.

Additionally, Basel III adopted three new capital surcharges (or buffers) on top of the base requirements. One buffer that applies to all banks is the capital conservation buffer under which banking organizations must maintain common equity Tier 1 capital equal to 2.5 percentage points above the minimum requirements to avoid restrictions on capital distributions (dividends and stock repurchases). Second, banks that are classified as Globally Systemic Important Banks (GSIBs) must maintain an additional second buffer to reduce the risk they pose to the financial system. A revision to Basel III in 2014, Basel Committee on Banking Supervision (2014), provides a formula for estimating the systemic importance of a bank and the resulting estimates are then translated into a required capital buffer that ranges from 1 percentage point to 3.5 percentage points. Third, Basel III provides bank supervisors with the authority to impose a countercyclical capital buffer of anywhere from zero to 2.5 percentage points to be implemented at national discretion.[9]

Although the United States has agreed to adopt Basel III as a minimum capital requirement, the US requirements will go beyond Basel III in a variety of ways. One important difference is that Section 171 of the DFA, called the Collins Amendment, requires that US banking organizations to remain compliant with all capital standards in effect before the passage of DFA. Among the standards that will remain in effect as minimum requirements for all US banks are Basel I and the 2010 version of the minimum leverage requirements.

The US requirements for the largest banks go even further, imposing requirements beyond those set by Basel III requirements in several important respects. First the United States added a second formula for calculating the systemic importance of a GSIB which incorporates the bank's reliance on wholesale funding and increases the maximum potential surcharge to 4.5 of risk-weighted assets.[10] The required GSIB

---

[9] The version of Basel III adopted by the United States includes provisions for a countercyclical buffer but the Federal Reserve is still considering how best to implement such a requirement.

[10] The surcharges are published in the Federal Register of August 14, 2015 and are available at www.gpo.gov/fdsys/pkg/FR-2015-08-14/pdf/2015–18702.pdf.

capital buffer is then the larger of that obtained from the Basel III formula and the formula that includes wholesale funding.

Second, the US version of the supplemental capital ratio differs in two important ways for US banks with more than $700 billion in consolidated total assets or more than $10 trillion in assets under custody. First, these banks must use daily average assets rather than the average of month-end assets, which reduce their ability to engage in window dressing to reduce their capital requirements. Second, these banks must maintain a leverage buffer greater than 2 percentage points above the Basel III minimum supplementary leverage ratio requirement of 3 percent.[11]

Finally, US bank holding companies with more than $50 billion in assets are required to conduct an annual stress test using three scenarios as a part of the Federal Reserve's Comprehensive Capital Analysis and Review (CCAR) process.[12] In order to pass this test, the bank holding companies must demonstrate that they could continue normal operations throughout the "severely adverse scenario." The severely adverse scenario in CCAR requires bank holding companies (BHCs) to estimate the effect of a significant recession over a three-year horizon. In order to be able to demonstrate their continued ability to operate through these scenarios, the BHC must remain in compliance with the regulatory capital requirements without reducing its supply of loans.[13]

Banks that fail CCAR will be told that the Federal Reserve objects to their capital plans, which means the BHC may not make any capital distribution (dividend or stock repurchase) without express authorization by the Federal Reserve. Given the perceived high cost of a Federal Reserve objection, banks seek to maintain a capital buffer above their regulatory minimums sufficient to pass the stress test.[14]

---

[11] Federal Reserve capital requirements are available at 12 CFR 217. A discussion of the revised rules and the modifications to the regulation are published in the Federal Register of September 26, 2014 and are available at www.gpo.gov/fdsys/pkg/FR-2014-09-26/pdf/2014–22083.pdf.

[12] See Wall (2014a, b) for more discussion of CCAR and its relationship to Basel III.

[13] Bank holding companies must also pass a qualitative review of their capital planning process in order to pass the test. See Board of Governors of the Federal Reserve System (2016) for a summary of the 2016 CCAR results.

[14] Some other supervisors also require their largest banks to undergo a stress, most notably the European Banking Authority. However, unlike the 2016 US

An important question for the GSIBs has been whether they will need to include the GSIB capital buffer in their minimum capital requirements for the CCAR stress tests. Thus far the minimum requirements for the purposes of the stress tests have not included the capital conservation or GSIB capital buffers. However, Tracy and Reilly (2016) recently reported that Federal Reserve governors Daniel Tarullo and Jerome Powell have indicated that the Federal Reserve probably will include the GSIB capital requirement in future stress tests.

Although the US standards generally require the same or more capital than international standards, the US requirements are weaker in one important way. The US accounting rules for derivatives allow reported exposures to be netted to a substantially greater degree than is permitted under the International Financial Reporting Standards (IFRS) that is used in most of the rest of the world. As a result, the largest US banks report significantly higher leverage ratios than would be the case under IFRS.[15]

3.3 Accounting

The accounting authorities also play an important role in capital adequacy regulation because the Basel risk-based ratios, the leverage ratio, and stress tests all use financial accounting definitions to calculate compliance with regulatory requirements. Two weaknesses in financial accounting were made especially apparent during the crisis: (1) important exposures were not revealed in some bank's financial statements because of weaknesses in the rules allowing the exclusion of qualifying special purpose vehicles (SPVs, also called special purpose entities), and (2) the rules for accounting for loan losses allowed for "too little, too late" recognition of credit losses.

CCAR, the European Banking Authority (2016) said it did not have a pass/fail threshold.

[15] The Federal Deposit Insurance Corporation estimates what US bank leverage would be under IFRS as a part of its "Global Capital Index." The December 2015 report finds that the average leverage ratio of the eight US banks classified as G-SIBs would decline over 2 percentage points to 5.97 percent. The December 2015 report is available at www.fdic.gov/about/learn/board/hoenig/capitalizationratios4q15.pdf.

3.3.1 Accounting for Special-Purpose Vehicles

Banks sponsored special-purpose vehicles (SPVs) to profit from the spread between the interest that could be earned on the more highly rated tranches of subprime and alt-A mortgage-backed securities and interest that would have to be paid to fund these purchases with asset backed commercial paper (ABCP). An important consideration in structuring these SPVs (or ABCP programs) was minimizing the increase in the sponsor's regulatory capital requirements, as banks perceive capital to be a higher cost source of funds. SPVs were legally separate entities from their sponsor, which facilitated the sponsor's attempts to avoid capital regulation but two other issues had to be addressed.

The first issue arose because ABCP buyers wanted additional protection against the risk of loss. If the sponsor provided an explicit credit guarantee, that would have substantially increased the sponsor's regulatory capital requirements. Acharya, Schnabl and Suarez (2013) show that the solution adopted by many sponsors was to structure their support as short-term liquidity guarantees that carried no capital charge under Basel I or II, but that de facto would serve as credit guarantees.

The second issue was whether the parent could avoid consolidating the SPV for the purposes of calculating regulatory capital ratios. The answer to this question varied depending on the home country of the sponsor that established both the financial accounting rules for consolidation and the regulatory rules for inclusion in the capital requirements.

Most countries in 2007 were either on or committed to following the International Financial Reporting Standards (IFRS). The approach taken in IFRS is to lay out the principles that should guide accounting choices rather than a detailed set of rules. IFRS principles for including (or consolidating) SPVs in their financial statement sheets would generally have forced sponsors to include the SPV's assets on their balance sheets. However, Thiemann (2012) points out that not all accounting authorities and bank supervisors in countries committed to IFRS had made IFRS mandatory for bank regulatory accounting purposes. He observes that in both France and Spain the supervisory authorities used their influence over accounting standards to enforce a strict version of IFRS that effectively prevented their banks from using SPVs to avoid capital regulation. However, in Germany the bank capital requirements were based on German accounting principles developed before IFRS and that allowed such SPVs. As a result, some German banks sponsored SPVs that ultimately led to losses for these banks.

US generally accepted accounting principles (GAAP) followed a more rule based approach which allowed the US corporation Enron to use SPVs to issue highly misleading financial statements prior to October 2001. However, after the discovery of Enron's use of SPVs, the accounting standards were tightened in December 2003, which required many ABCP programs to be consolidated on their sponsors' balance sheets. The effect of this change on bank capital requirements was largely undone by changes in the bank capital regulation. The supervisors changed the rules in 2004 to allow ABCP programs that were being consolidated for financial accounting purposes to be excluded for the purposes of meeting the regulators' risk-based capital requirements.

Post-crisis revisions to IFRS and to US GAAP strengthened their guidance on SPVs according to Papa (2013).[16] Additionally, the bank supervisors eliminated their loopholes that allowed ABCP programs to be excluded from the calculation of regulatory capital requirements.[17] These revisions should make it almost impossible for banks to use SPVs to take additional risk without a commensurate increase in their regulatory capital requirements.

3.3.2 Loan Loss Accounting

Both IFRS and GAAP required firms to report their losses using the incurred credit loss model prior to the crisis. This model would permit losses to be recognized only to the extent that there was evidence prior to the reporting date that the loan had become impaired. Banks used this requirement during the crisis to argue that insufficient evidence of impairment existed and, hence, no loss should be recognized. After the crisis, many viewed the incurred loss model as being responsible for bank loan loss provisioning being "too little, too late."

---

[16] See Financial Accounting Standards Board (2009) for the change in US financial accounting standards

[17] A description of the change in US regulations may be found at www.gpo.gov/fdsys/pkg/FR-2010-01-28/pdf/2010-825.pdf.

After the crisis, both IFRS and US GAAP have been revised to versions of the expected credit losses model, which requires earlier loss recognition. The Financial Accounting Standard Board (2016) announced that US GAAP will be based on the stricter version of expected credit losses, requiring that the loan loss allowance reflect the full amount of the expected losses over the lifetime of the loan. As a result of this requirement, banks will be required to recognize expected credit losses from the moment they acquire the loan even if there is no new information suggesting the loan has become riskier.[18]

Critics of the US approach argued that such loss recognition was inconsistent with the amortized cost model that is otherwise used as the basis of accounting for loans. In an effort to retain the expected credit loss model without requiring additional provisions when a loan was made, IFRS broke loans into two categories based on whether the credit risk of the loan (or group of loans) has increased significantly since the loan was first recorded according to EY (2014). If there has not been a significant increase, the lender must recognize the expected credit losses on the loan only over the next twelve months. However, if there has been a significant increase, the lender must recognize the lifetime expected credit losses.

3.4 Liquidity

Although supervisors have long been concerned about their banks' liquidity position, liquidity had not been subject to internationally agreed minimum numerical regulatory standards similar to that of capital. Basel III changed this by setting two minimum requirements for liquidity.

One of the new Basel III requirements, the Liquidity Coverage Ratio (LCR), requires large banking organizations to maintain high-quality liquid assets (HQLAs) at least equal to their projected net cash outflows over a stressful thirty-day period. The other requirement, the Net Stable Funding Ratio (NSFR) imposes similar requirements over a one-year horizon. Both the LCR and NSFR apply weights to liabilities that reflect the risk of their running within the specified time horizon and to assets to reflect the ease with which they can be used to meet maturing obligations.

---

[18] See Wall (2013) for a discussion of the change in FASB's impairment standard.

The United States has adopted regulations implementing the LCR and is working on regulations implementing the NSFR.[19] The full version of the US LCR regulation applies to all banking organizations with more than $250 billion in assets or $10 billion or more on-balance sheet foreign exposure or BHCs with subsidiary depository institutions with assets of $10 billion or more. A less stringent, modified version applies to bank holding companies that do not meet the aforementioned thresholds but have $50 billion or more in total assets.

The full version of the LCR is somewhat more stringent than that required by Basel III. Among the differences according to Davis Polk (2014) are that under the US calculations: (1) certain assets receive less favorable liquidity weightings, and (2) the US formula includes a penalty for cash inflow and outflow mismatches within the thirty-day horizon.[20]

On the supervisory side, the Federal Reserve has adopted the Comprehensive Liquidity Analysis and Review (CLAR) as the liquidity review similar to its use of the CCAR for reviewing capital.[21] The CLAR, like the CCAR, is a forward looking, horizontal assessment of the largest banks liquidity position and management processes.

3.5 Compensation

A survey published by the Institute for International Finance (2009) found that even the banks agreed incentive compensation structures were a problem, with 98 percent of the large international banks participating in the survey saying that compensation structures were a factor in the financial crisis of 2007 and 2008. Although incentive compensation practices varied across banks and even within banks, in

---

[19] The Federal Deposit Insurance Corporation, Federal Reserve and Office of the Comptroller of the Currency adopted the LCR. The requirement is incorporated into Federal Reserve liquidity regulation as a part of 12 CFR 249, available at www.gpo.gov/fdsys/pkg/FR-2014-10-10/pdf/2014–22520.pdf. The same regulatory agencies issued a proposal for the NSFR that is available at www.federalreserve.gov/newsevents/press/bcreg/bcreg20160503a1.pdf

[20] http://usbasel3.com/docs/Final%20LCR%20Visual%20Memo.pdf.

[21] Federal Reserve governor Tarullo (2014) provides an overview of Federal Reserve regulation of liquidity, including the CLAR program.

general these practices tended not to risk adjust the earnings used in allocating incentive compensation. In an effort to address this problem, the Financial Stability Board (2009) and the US bank supervisors issued guidelines for sound compensation practices.[22]

In general, the US supervisory guidelines take the view that the extent to which a bank uses incentive compensation should be determined by its board of directors but that sound compensation practices require that any compensation based on an employee's contribution to earnings should reflect the risk taken to generate that return. One way of taking account of the risks would be to use risk-adjusted returns, such as risk adjusting a trader's earnings for the risk it creates for the bank. However, such an approach may not provide adequate risk adjustment for some employees whose decisions may impact the firm over a period of many years, such as senior bank management. In these cases, one alternative is to require that some portion of the incentive compensation remain at risk after it was initially awarded. For example, the employee could be granted stock that vests over a three-year period. If it becomes apparent that the grants were based on excessive risk taking, the amount of stock issued could be reduced to reflect the new information about the employee's risk taking.

Many other developed countries have adopted similar supervisory guidance or rules. The European Union took the view that compensating employees primarily through incentive compensation was itself a problem. Thus, the European Union's Capital Directive IV not only applies the FSB principles but also limits incentive compensation no more than 100 percent of the base salary (or in some cases 200 percent with the shareholders' approval).[23]

---

[22] The US supervisory guidance and a related discussion are published in the Federal Register of July 25, 2010 and are available at www.gpo.gov/fdsys/pkg/FR-2010-06-25/pdf/2010–15435.pdf. Shortly before these guidelines were passed, Section 956 of the Dodd–Frank Act directed bank regulators to work with other federal financial regulatory agencies, including the Securities and Exchange Commission (SEC) to issue a new rule applicable to banks and some nonbank financial firms that prohibits incentive-based payments that encourage inappropriate risks. A draft of the proposed rule was issued for comment on June 10, 2016 and is available at www.federalreserve.gov/newsevents/press/bcreg/bcreg20160516a1.pdf.

[23] See Article 75 of the Directive, available at http://eur-lex.europa.eu/legal-content/EN/TXT/?uri=CELEX:32013L0036.

48   *Larry D. Wall*

3.6 Reduce Exposure to Financial Market Risk

An important source of revenue and risk for the large banks prior to the crisis was their involvement in over-the-counter (OTC) derivatives and more generally in wholesale financial markets. Measures have been taken along both dimensions since the crisis.

3.6.1 OTC Derivatives

One of the concerns that emerged during the crisis was that the largest banks were becoming so interconnected that allowing one to fail would endanger others. The poster child for this problem was American International Group (AIG), which had sold credit protection through credit default swaps to a large number of banks. Shortly after the Lehman Brothers failure, AIG was rescued from failure by the Federal Reserve in large part because of concern over the systemic consequences of letting it fail given its outstanding book of credit default swaps.

Concern about OTC derivatives became so acute that the G-7 Leaders' Statement from their 2009 meeting in Pittsburgh explicitly called for these contracts to be centrally cleared where appropriate and for higher capital requirements on those contracts that are not centrally cleared. The United States followed through on this commitment with Title VII of the DFA mandating the clearing of actively traded contracts and requiring the appropriate federal financial regulatory body to impose capital requirements on contracts that are not cleared.

3.6.2 Proprietary Trading

The large US banking organizations were major participants in domestic and many foreign capital markets prior to the crisis. The returns from capital market activities tend to be more volatile. In response to concerns that some capital market activities posed excessive risk to banking organizations Section 619 of the DFA banned proprietary trading and restricted bank ownership of hedge funds and private equity funds. This section of DFA is often referred to as the Volcker Act in honor of former Federal Reserve chairman Paul Volcker.[24]

---

[24] The Volcker Rule is implemented as a part of 12 CFR 351. The regulation and a related discussion of it by the regulatory agencies was published in the

The United Kingdom took a somewhat different approach to containing the risk from its investment banking operations. The United Kingdom has mandated that the banks ringfence (or legally and operationally separate) their domestic retail banking operations from their wholesale banking operations.[25] The EU has proposed a rule that is similar in intent to the US rule.[26]

3.7 Limiting Size and Complexity

One of the concerns that was raised during the writing of the DFA is that the size and complexity of the largest US banks make them more difficult to supervise and, if one should fail, makes it more difficult to resolve. Thus, the DFA contains new provisions designed to limit bank's ability to grow via mergers. The Act also gives the supervisors some ability to force banks to become smaller and less complex if that is necessary to allow them to be resolved.

3.7.1 Limits on Bank Size

Competition authorities and bank supervisors have long had some ability to block mergers on the grounds that the combined banks would have too much market power or would be too risky. BHCs in the United States have been required prior approval by the Federal Reserve and Department of Justice before they could undertake a merger. The antitrust component of this review has long focused on local geographic markets in which retail and small business customers could obtain banking services. Thus, competition law in the United States prevented local oligopolies but did little to prevent large banks from growing larger by entering new markets. However, the federal law authorizing interstate banking and branching, the Riegle–Neal

---

Federal Register of January 31, 2014 and is available at www.gpo.gov/fdsys/pkg/FR-2014-01-31/pdf/2013-31511.pdf.

[25] www.bankofengland.co.uk/pra/Pages/supervision/structuralrefor proprietary trading m/default.aspx

[26] The European Commission webpage devoted to banking structural reform is available at http://ec.europa.eu/finance/bank/structural-reform/index_en.htm. An earlier report on reforming EU banking structure, Liikanen (2012), proposed ringfencing similar to that mandated by the United Kingdom.

Interstate Banking and Branching Efficiency Act of 1994 contained a provision that prohibited the acquisition of bank if the resulting banking organization would have more than 10 percent of deposit of nationwide deposits.

The DFA also imposed a new quantitative limit and gave the supervisors added authority to reject bank takeovers. Section 622 of the Act prohibits an acquisition of a financial company if the resulting financial company has more than 10 percent of the aggregate consolidated liabilities of all financial companies. Additionally, Section 604(e) of the Act requires that the "risk to the stability of the United States banking or financial system" be considered as a part of the merger review process.[27]

3.7.2 Living Wills

Prior to the crisis, banks were generally not responsible for developing plans for their own resolution. This changed in the United States with the passage of the DFA in 2010. This was followed by guidance from the Financial Stability Board (2014) which sets out the core elements the FSB regards as necessary for effective resolution of globally systemically important financial institutions (G-SIFI) without taxpayer exposure to loss.

Some of the most advanced and well publicized work has occurred in the US Section 165(d) of the DFA that requires banking organizations with assets of more than $50 billion and nonbank SIFIs to prepare a resolution plan (widely referred to as a "living will"). This living will is supposed to provide a sort of roadmap that would allow the organization to be resolved under existing bankruptcy law (including FDIC resolution of any insured depository subsidiaries). Moreover, to the extent that better planning is not by itself sufficient to develop a satisfactory resolution plan, banks are expected to make any operational and structural changes needed to produce such a plan.

The largest banks in the United States have gone through several rounds of submissions starting in 2013. These proposals have been reviewed jointly by the Federal Reserve and the FDIC and the two

---

[27] For further discussion of the financial stability standard, see Capital One Financial Corporation, FRB Order 2012-2 (February 14, 2012), available at www.federalreserve.gov/newsevents/press/orders/order20120214.pdf.

agencies have focused particular attention on the resolution plans of eight large, complex banking organizations.[28] The Board of Governors of the Federal Reserve and Federal Deposit Insurance Corporation (2016) review of the submissions by these eight banks highlighted several deficiencies in banks' existing plans including their complex legal structure.[29]

The DFA and the regulatory agencies recognized that resolution planning was a new requirement and developing satisfactory plans would take time. However, the DFA authorizes the Federal Reserve and FDIC to order a banking group to divest certain activities to make the group easier to resolve if the group proves unable to develop a satisfactory plan.

3.8 Conclusion

The United States has strengthened its system of bank prudential regulation in a variety of ways since the crisis. In part these changes have been made in coordination with international standard setting bodies. However, the United States has often adopted stricter versions of the international agreements and has also taken action on some issues not covered by international standards.

References

Acharya, V. V., Schnabl, P., and Suarez, G. (2013). Securitization without risk transfer. *Journal of Financial Economics*, 107(3), 515–536.

Bair, Sheila (2007). Remarks to the 2007 Risk Management and Allocation Conference, Paris, June 25. Available at www.fdic.gov/news/news/speeches/archives/2007/chairman/spjun2507.html.

Basel Committee on Banking Supervision (1988). International convergence of capital measurement and capital standards (July). Available at www.bis.org/publ/bcbs04a.htm.

Basel Committee on Banking Supervision (2004). Basel II: International Convergence of Capital Measurement and Capital Standards: A Revised Framework (June). Available at www.bis.org/publ/bcbs107.htm.

---

[28] These organizations are Bank of America, Bank of New York Mellon, Citigroup, Goldman Sachs, JPMorgan Chase, Morgan Stanley, State Street, and Wells Fargo.

[29] Report available at www.federalreserve.gov/newsevents/press/bcreg/bcreg20160413a2.pdf.

Basel Committee on Banking Supervision (2010). Basel III: A global regulatory framework for more resilient banks and banking systems (December). Available at www.bis.org/publ/bcbs189_dec2010.htm.

Basel Committee on Banking Supervision 2014). The G-SIB assessment methodology – score calculation. (November). Available at www.bis.org/bcbs/publ/d296.pdf.

Board of Governors of the Federal Reserve System (2016). Comprehensive capital analysis and review 2016: Assessment framework and results (June). Available at www.federalreserve.gov/newsevents/press/bcreg/bcreg20160629a1.pdf.

Board of Governors of the Federal Reserve System, Federal Deposit Insurance Corporation, Office of the Comptroller of the Currency, and Office of Thrift Supervision (2006). Summary findings of the Fourth Quantitative Impact Study. Available at www.federalreserve.gov/newsevents/press/bcreg/20060224aa.htm.

European Banking Authority (2014). EBA guidelines on sound remuneration policies (December 21). Available at www.eba.europa.eu/documents/10180/1314839/EBA-GL-2015–22+Guidelines+on+Sound+Remuneration+Policies.pdf/1b0f3f99-f913-461a-b3e9-fa0064b1946b.

European Banking Authority (2016). 2016 EU-wide stress test results (July 29). Available at http://storage.eba.europa.eu/documents/10180/1532819/2016-EU-wide-stress-test-Results.pdf.

EY (2014). Impairment of financial instruments under IFRS 9 (December). Available at www.ey.com/Publication/vwLUAssets/Applying_IFRS:_Impairment_of_financial_instruments_under_IFRS_9/$FILE/Apply-FI-Dec2014.pdf.

Financial Accounting Standards Board (2009). FASB Issues Statements 166 and 167 Pertaining to Securitizations and Special Purpose Entities. News Release 06/12/09. Available at www.fasb.org/cs/ContentServer?pagename=FASB/FASBContent_C/NewsPage&cid=1176156240834.

Financial Accounting Standards Board (2016). Financial Instruments – Credit Losses (Topic 326), Measurement of Credit Losses on Financial Instruments (June). No. 2016-13. Available at www.fasb.org/jsp/FASB/Document_C/DocumentPage?cid=1176168232528

Financial Stability Board (2009). FSB principles for sound compensation practices: Implementation standards. (September 25). Available at www.financialstabilityboard.org/wp-content/uploads/r_090925c.pdf.

Financial Stability Board (2014). Key attributes of effective resolution regimes. (October). Available at www.fsb.org/wp-content/uploads/r_141015.pdf.

G-7, (2009). Leaders' Statement, the Pittsburgh Summit (September 24–25). Available at www.treasury.gov/resource-center/international/g7-g20/Documents/pittsburgh_summit_leaders_statement_250909.pdf.

Institute of International Finance. (2009) Compensation in financial services: Industry progress and the agenda for change. (March). Available at www.iif.com/file/7101/download?token=xsksV4yg.

Liikanen, E. (2012). High-level Expert Group on reforming the structure of the EU banking sector. Final Report, Brussels, 2. Available at http://ec.europa.eu/internal_market/bank/docs/high-level_expert_group/report_en.pdf.

Papa, V. (2013). Assessing financial reporting transparency of securitization transactions. CFA Institute. Available at https://blogs.cfainstitute.org/marketintegrity/2013/08/09/assessing-financial-reporting-transparency-of-securitization-transactions/.

Polk, Davis (2014). U.S. Basel III liquidity coverage ratio final rule visual memorandum (September 23). Available at http://usbasel3.com/docs/Final%20LCR%20Visual%20Memo.pdf.

Tarullo, D. K. (2014). Liquidity regulation. Speech given at the Clearing House 2014 Annual Conference, New York, New York (November 20). Available at www.federalreserve.gov/newsevents/speech/tarullo2014 1120a%20.htm.

Thiemann, Matthias (2012). "Out of the shadows?" Accounting for Special Purpose Entities in European banking systems. *Competition & Change* 16:1, 37–55.

Tracy, Ryan and David Reilly (2016). Fed governors signal bigger bank capital requirements looming. *Wall Street Journal*, June 2.

United States Government Accountability Office (2013). Financial crisis losses and potential impacts of the Dodd–Frank Act. GAO-13–180 (January 16). Available at www.gao.gov/products/GAO-13-180.

Wall, L. D. (2010). Too big to fail after FDICIA. Federal Reserve Bank of Atlanta Economic Review, 95(1), I. Available at https://frbatlanta.org/-/media/Documents/research/publications/economic-review/2010/vol95no1_wall.pdf.

(2013). FASB proposes (too?) early loan loss recognition, Federal Reserve Bank of Atlanta Notes from the Vault (April). Available at www.frbatlanta.org/cenfis/publications/notesfromthevault/1308.cfm.

(2014a) Measuring capital adequacy supervisory stress tests in a Basel world. *Journal of Financial Perspectives* 2:1, 85–94.

(2014b). The adoption of stress testing: Why the Basel capital measures were not enough. *Journal of Banking Regulation* 15: 266–276.

4 | Notes on the Interaction between Financial Markets and the Macroeconomy: Financial Markets and Policy through the Lens of Macroeconomics

JOUKO VILMUNEN

4.1 Introduction

During the post-2008 period much has been written about Dynamic Stochastic General Equilibrium (DSGE) models, which have come to play a dominant role in macroeconomic research. During the same period DSGE macroeconomists have come under heavy criticism from various sources. One of the most severe criticisms has perhaps come from the profession itself, namely from Paul Romer,[1] who basically says that for the last thirty years there has been very little, if any, progress in macroeconomics and that the field has gone in a completely wrong direction. Romer argues that unverified assumptions and even assumptions at odds with empirical microeconomic evidence are often employed by mainstream macroeconomists and that these assumptions are hidden deep in the DSGE structure. Romer is in favour of evidence-based macroeconomic modelling and calls for realism in the basic modelling assumptions.[2] He does not subscribe to Milton Friedman's methodological dictum that instead of the realism of a model's assumptions, it is the consistency of its predictions with the data that makes it a good model.

Before going further, one thing should be made clear: there is no standard DSGE model, but the field of DSGE macroeconomics is very

---

[1] See his writings on https://paulromer.net/.
[2] Narayana Kocherlakota has also argued along these lines, https://sites.google
.com/site/kocherlakota009/home/research

The usual disclaimer applies: the views expressed in this article do not necessarily reflect those of the Bank of Finland.

diverse. As Anton Korinek (2015, 2) rightly emphasizes, many modern macroeconomists who employ the DSGE approach – including the author of this chapter – have an appreciation of the deep methodological concerns and challenges incorporated in the approach and are actually working hard on addressing these challenges to expand the frontier of our knowledge. Similar thinking is echoed in Olivier Blanchard's writings on DSGE approach (Blanchard 2016a, b).

In this chapter I discuss my views on macroprudential policy and financial regulation. As I am (mostly) a macroeconomist, I will look into these issues through the lens of monetary macroeconomics and, in particular, of monetary policy. The mainstream modelling framework – DSGE approach to macroeconomics – has a special role, both implicitly and explicitly. I will start, in the next section, by discussing systemic risks, because after the 2007–2009 financial crisis these risks feature prominently in policy debates and because a growing academic literature suggests models for analysing and measuring systemic risks as well as the associated financial and macroeconomic stability problems. The discussion is heavily influenced by Lars Peter Hansen's recent writings (see, in particular, Hansen 2012). I will then go on to discuss the DSGE approach to macroeconomics. I have chosen this order because most critics of the DSGE approach base their arguments on the failure of the DSGE models – at least in their current vintage – to predict systemic events such as financial crises and to give appropriate policy advice to manage and resolve them. Section 4.4 discusses financial frictions and monetary policy and Section 4.5 summarizes by mulling with idea that maybe we should think of the DSGE approach to macroeconomics as a long-term research aim rather than the principal research lab to test ideas on e.g. financial frictions, financial crises and the associated (optimal) policies.

4.2 Systemic Risk or Systemic Uncertainty

Debate over public oversight of financial institutions – systemically important (SI) institutions in particular – often makes reference to *systemic risk* as a rationale for prudent policymaking. One could argue that this is understandable, because an SI financial institution, by being too big, too interconnected or, from the point of view of the *system*, by misbehaving can impose considerable costs on the financial system and the aggregate economy. History testifies that all the major crises involve large monetary and welfare costs on economies experiencing sudden stops of the financial system.

However, systemic risk is still a relatively poorly understood and measured concept. One could then ask whether systemic risk should be an explicit target for measurement or relegated to being a buzz word used to rationalize regulatory discretion (Hansen 2012, 1). To give some benchmark, compare systemic and *systematic*, where the latter is well studied and supported by extensive modelling and measurement. Systemic risk is something different, referring to major disruption in the financial system. But it is not well measured: for example Bisias, Flood and Valavanis (2012) identify thirty-one ways to measure systemic risk. In any case, given that systemic risk is poorly understood, there is no off-the-shelf model that we can use to measure it.

Hence, we are bound to use coarse approximation in measuring systemic risk, at least in the short run. But then we have to be concerned about and raise some scepticism in our probabilistic measurement of systemic risk (Hansen 2012, 6). This is not about models being right or wrong, as all models are by their very nature wrong. All models simplify and abstract, which means that all sorts of gaps remain. This, in turn, suggests it is important to know which of the gaps are non-trivial and which are negligible. If we suspect that some of the gaps are non-trivial, we are back to the question of how to express scepticism (Hansen 2012, 6).

If we accept the proposition that systemic risk is a poorly understood and measured concept and that there are no off-the-self solutions to guide one's intuition in modelling and measuring it, we must conclude that any effort to general equilibrium analysis incorporating systemic risk issues may be a daunting task involving critical restrictions on alternative ways of modelling systemic risk. We will return to this point in the next section, when we discuss DSGE models more closely.

But before engaging in that discussion, I feel the need to highlight one further aspect raised by Hansen (2012), namely that simple models, although incomplete along some dimensions can provide powerful insights. However, the problem becomes one of wanting to know how to embrace such models while acknowledging scepticism that should justifiably go along with them (Hansen 2012, 6–7). This is an enduring problem in the use of DSGE models and it seems unavoidable as we confront the important task of building models designed to measure systemic risk. The high hope is that we can make progress here. However, we need to abandon the presumption that we can measure systemic *risk* and go after the conceptually more difficult notion of quantifying systemic (Knightian) *uncertainty*.

4.3 DSGE Approach to Macroeconomics

The DSGE approach is basically a research methodology for the field of macroeconomics. As such it defines the general strategy that researchers are supposed to apply to research questions in macroeconomics, defines how research is to be conducted and identifies a set of methods and restrictions on what is permissible in macroeconomics (Korinek 2015, 2). Korinek distinguishes two types of methodological restrictions imposed by the DSGE approach, conceptual restrictions and quantitative methods and restrictions. The former involve such issues as the requirement for models to be dynamic, stochastic and general equilibrium, the use of microfoundations and the analysis of stationary equilibria (Korinek 2015, 2).

Korinek (2015) analyses the benefits and costs of each of these restrictions. Without repeating them all, I will highlight only those that I think are the most important ones for my purpose. First, focusing on stationary or ergodic equilibria may be problematic, as many real-world processes need not follow a defined ergodic distribution. Furthermore, if the economy is assumed always to revert back to a well-behaved steady state, there is less concern about the destabilizing dynamics than there may be in the real world: why bother about financial crises?

Second, general equilibrium macroeconomic models need to be built from the bottom up on solid microeconomic foundations. Korinek (2015) argues forcefully (p. 4) and gives examples that there are many sciences that apply different methodological approaches at the micro- and macrolevel. These sciences assume approximate laws at the macrolevel, although they are not necessarily derivable from underlying micro-foundations. Macrophenomena or 'emergent phenomena' are the outcome of dynamically interacting entities at the micro-level. Agent-based models in economics build on this idea of dynamic interaction between different agents at the microlevel. On the other hand, this also means that the behaviour of the macroeconomy cannot be reduced to the behaviour of individuals at the microlevel. As an example, consider the concept of aggregate demand: as an emergent phenomenon in macroeconomics it is difficult to trace it back to its precise micro origin. So the lesson seems to be that different methodological approaches in microeconomics and macroeconomics seem desirable: they could actually inform each other and learn from each other.

Third, Korinek (2015) discusses rational expectations and Lucas-critique as part of the microfoundations. Naturally neither one of these is a defining feature of DSGE models, but they apply more generally. Note, however, that rational expectations are not a part of the parcel of optimizing behaviour at the individual level: they apply at the market (i.e. aggregate) level. It is the representative agent assumption that hides this feature. In any case, the Lucas critique is as reliable as the underlying (macro)model.

In the context of the quantitative restrictions imposed by the DSGE approach, Korinek (2015) focuses particularly on the practice of building a quantitative DSGE model under a defined set of shocks and, after calibration and possibly estimation, of showing that the model can replicate the chosen, typically second moments in the data. But the criterion of matching moments may provide a highly misleading guide for real-world policies: for example, second moments do not well capture important macroeconomic events, such as financial crises, as these are tail events. Hence, a good model of financial crises may not gain its reputation by matching moments used to evaluate regular business cycle models, which are driven by a different set of shocks (see Korinek 2015, 8).

4.4 DSGE Models, Financial Frictions and Monetary Policy

Being able to (theoretically) analyse the interaction between financial market disruptions and the macroeconomy requires more than what most of the current DSGE models can handle. Many of the DSGE models are well suited for econometric estimation and they measure the consequences of different shocks as well as model explicitly the transmission mechanisms for these shocks. However, these models are typically 'small shocks' models using local approximations. Hence, in order to analyse crisis times (e.g. when critical constraints bind), we are bound to use separate local approximations, if we want to follow the standard modelling strategy. Fortunately, however, some progress in this respect has been made, e.g. by Gertler and Kiyotaki (2015).

Recent advances in DSGE modelling have only scratched the surface on how to extend these models to improve our understanding of the macroeconomic consequences of upheavals in financial markets – and to improve the quality of policy advice. A host of open research questions remains (Walsh 2010):

1. How best to model financial constraints, both in terms of a theoretical basis and empirical relevance?
2. How best to characterize the macroeconomic consequences of crisis related shocks that are large and infrequent?
3. How best to model the origin of these shocks?
4. How best to model the consequences of financial constraints or frictions to the trade-off faced by policymakers, especially central banks?
   a. Financial frictions affect monetary policy transmission and generate distortions in the real economy.
   b. Financial frictions also interact with price rigidities, thus affecting the conventional policy trade-offs.

However, it is not obvious that monetary policy is the most efficient instrument for mitigating the effects of financial shocks. Time-varying and targeted financial regulation is a better instrument for this purpose in the similar sense that time-varying tax and subsidies may constitute better tools to deal with mark-up shocks. However, if regulation fails to do the job, central banks cannot ignore financial frictions and financial stability. Furthermore, financial disturbances in this case may force central banks to make trade-offs in their inflation and output objectives.

So, what is the best research agenda to follow in seeking answers to the above questions? One based on the DSGE approach? Or something else? As noted earlier, the DSGE approach imposes fairly stringent constraints on macroeconomic modelling, as also noted by some of its critics. However, many of the critics of DSGE macroeconomics agree that it is, in principle, desirable for macroeconomic models to incorporate dynamics, to study general equilibrium effects and to deal with stochastic uncertainty. Consequently, critics seem to refer to broader methodological concerns about modern macroeconomics. One of these concerns relates to the inherent complexity of

DSGE models – apart, perhaps, from the three-equation toy model of the New Keynesian type. Complexity has the potential of restricting the scope of the analysis carried out by DSGE models, which in turn implies that the set of ideas that we can describe rigorously using quantitative DSGE models may be smaller than the set using simpler models. In particular, methodological restrictions imposed by DSGE approach may force us to formalize new ideas in a way that is potentially of no help in understanding the corresponding real world phenomena. This brings me back to financial frictions and concluding words.

4.5 Summarizing: Modelling Financial Frictions, Need for More Methodological Diversity and Out-of-Box Thinking

I must confess that I am a DSGE enthusiast. However, I would like to endorse DSGE modelling in macroeconomics more as a long-term research aim. I am increasingly often troubled by the idea that maybe the DSGE framework does not provide macroeconomic researchers the ideal platform or laboratory to think about and test which financial frictions (and shocks they probably generate) are the most relevant ones for macroeconomy and what is the ideal way of modelling them in a macroeconomic context. As argued earlier, the DSGE approach to macroeconomics imposes methodological restrictions on modelling that may force a researcher to choose particular formalizations that e.g. bear little or no resemblance to the real-world phenomena that motivated the analysis in the first place. Or even worse so, we may choose or be forced to analyse only particular macroeconomic problems.

An example of the latter was the pre-2008 practice of building DSGE based business cycle models, which more often than not incorporated a unique ergodic steady state. Or, more accurately, macroeconomic researchers choose to focus on such equilibria, leaving no room for formal analysis of the emergence of financial crises and their macroeconomic implications. I am not sure whether we should condemn the DSGE approach for having not been able to predict the most recent financial crisis and to provide proper policy guidance or whether macroeconomists increasingly believed that financial crises belonged to the past in which case macroeconomics can focus on building dynamic models for normal business cycle analysis. Apart from Raghuram Rajan's famous Jackson Hole speech in 2005 (Rajan 2005), not too many economists overall, be it macroeconomists or others, talked about accumulating instabilities in the financial sector that if, and when, realized, will have extremely severe macroeconomic consequences.

It may be the case that we need more out-of-box thinking and methodological diversity in macroeconomics, in particular over the shorter run, to test new ideas and aim to model them using a full-fledged DSGE approach only ultimately, once we have found the best way to formalize them in a macroeconomic context. This is especially important when it comes to monetary policy objectives, which are potentially affected by various financial frictions and their interaction with price frictions. Central banks may play a big role on the demand side for such a research agenda for the natural reason that they already tend to use a set of models of different types in their macroeconomic analysis and forecasting. Central banks have already started to complete their set of models to improve the quality of macrofinance analysis conducted in these banks. New macroprudential policy responsibilities have forced central banks to move ahead to sharpen the analytical tools available to them. Future thus looks challenging and highly interesting.

References

Bisias, D., M. Flood, A.W. Lo and S. Valavanis (2012). A survey of systemic risk Analytics. Working Paper 0001. Washington, DC: Office of Financial Research.

Blanchard, O. (2016a). Do DSGE models have a future? Peterson Institute for International Economics (PIIE), PB16–11.

(2016b). Further thoughts on DSGE models. *Real Time Economic Issues Watch*, PIIE, October 2, 2016.

Gertler, M. and N. Kiyotaki (2015). Banking, liquidity and bank runs in an infinite horizon economy. *American Economic Review* 105:7, 2011–2043.

Hansen, L-P. (2012). Challenges in identifying and measuring systemic risk. NEBR Working Paper No. 18505. Cambridge, MA: National Bureau of Economic Research.

Korinek, A. (2015). Thoughts on DSGE macroeconomics: Matching the moments but missing the point? Available at www.korinek.com/.

Rajan, R. (2005). Has finance made the world riskier? In *The Greenspan Era: Lessons for the Future*. Federal Reserve Bank of Kansas City. Also published in *European Financial Management*, 12:4, 2006, 499–533.

Walsh, C. (2010). Using monetary policy to stabilize the economy. In Federal Reserve Bank of Kansas City, *Financial Stability and Macroeconomic Policy*. 2009 Jackson Hole Symposium, pp. 245–296.

5 | Investment Doctrines for Banks, from Real Bills to Post-Crisis Reforms

JUHA TARKKA

5.1 Introduction

This chapter offers a historical perspective on regulatory ideas of how banks should invest. A recurring theme in the development of bank lending doctrines is the relative weight given to liquidity on the one hand and solvency on the other. The emphasis between these aspects of bank assets has varied as the result of developments in central banking and the growth of money markets. Significant shifts of emphasis between liquidity and solvency have also often occurred after banking crises or other major events that have brought new problems to light.

Historically, attention first shifted from liquidity of the assets, which the early 'real bills' doctrine emphasised, to their marketability. Thereafter, the solidity (in the sense of the underlying value) of collateral gradually became the primary concern. This change resulted in the anticipated income doctrine of banking and the idea of liability management. In the decades following the Second World War, liquidity considerations were progressively displaced by credit risk management and the focus on capital adequacy. An accompanying trend was the increasing faith and reliance on the ability of money markets to provide liquidity to fundamentally solvent institutions. For a while, this trend seemed to make liquidity a subordinate concept, as if it were merely a consequence of solvency.

However, during the latest crisis severe disruptions in the functioning of money and capital markets were experienced. This has led to a less sanguine view of the functioning of the markets, and forced a reconsideration whereby bank managers and also regulators again emphasise the liquidity of bank portfolios.

5.2 The Real Bills Doctrine and Its Antecedents

The natural starting point for a discussion of the development of banking principles is the famous real bills doctrine. Because of its historical

importance, it constitutes a benchmark against which other investment doctrines of banks can be compared.

The real bills doctrine can be summarised as a requirement that
banks should practice only short-term lending, and that this lending
should be of a 'self-liquidating' nature. This doctrine is of enormous
importance in monetary history, being the predominant ideal of good
banking practice for most of the nineteenth century and remaining so
until the changes caused by the Great Depression and other monetary
upheavals of the early twentieth century.

The classic exposition of the real bills doctrine was given by Adam
Smith in his *The Wealth of Nations* of 1776. Smith can be often
regarded as the first exponent of the doctrine and soon became the
standard reference (Mints 1945, 25). The following famous passage
from *The Wealth of Nations* deserves being quoted in full (Smith
1991 269):

When a bank discounts to a merchant a *real bill of exchange* drawn by a
real creditor upon a real debtor, and which, as soon as it becomes due, is
really paid by that debtor; it only advances to him a part of the value which
he would otherwise be obliged to keep by him unemployed, and in ready
money for answering occasional demands. The payment of the bill, when
it becomes due, replaces to the bank the value of what it had advanced,
together with the interest. The coffers of the bank, so far as its dealings are
confined to such customers, resemble a water pond, from which, though
a stream is continually running out, yet another is continually running in,
fully equal to that which runs out; so that, without any further care or attention, the pond keeps always equally, or very near equally full. Little or no
expense can ever be necessary for replenishing the coffers of such a bank.

The passage is from Chapter 2 of Book II of *The Wealth of Nations*,
in which Smith discusses the effects of paper money (banknotes) and
compares the Scottish and English banking experience.

The term 'real bills' refers to a particular type of credit instrument: a
bill of exchange originating from financing a real transaction, namely
the sale of goods. This could be a sale of goods by a manufacturer to
a wholesaler, or by a wholesaler to a retailer, or possibly a purchase of
raw materials by a manufacturer. The use of real bills of exchange in
connection of foreign trade was also very important.

The real bill was written (drawn) by the seller of the goods and,
once signed (accepted) by the buyer, it constituted a promise of the

buyer to pay a given amount of money after a given time, usually in a few months. Typically, however, the seller would get the money before the due date by selling the bill (at a discount) to a bank, which would then become the ultimate creditor and would collect the money in due course. The safety of the bill from the bank's perspective was enhanced by the fact that both the drawer and the acceptor of a bill of exchange are responsible for payment to the bank. According to Smith, and the other proponents of the real bills doctrine, the asset portfolio of a prudently run bank should consist entirely or at least mainly of such discounted real bills.

An important reason why Smith and his followers considered bills of exchange to be the most suitable form of credit for banks to give was that he considered them to be 'self-liquidating'. This meant that the underlying transaction, financed by the bill, could be expected to generate the funds needed to pay the bill in time. For example, when the goods financed by the bill were resold, or when the raw materials purchased with a bill became a finished product and were sold, money would become available to pay the bill as it became due. Thus, customers being able to redeem their obligations, a bank with a steady portfolio of real bills could expect its liquidity to be stable as well.

The real bills doctrine reflects the priority given to liquidity in the composition of bank portfolios. It is intended to ensure that the asset position of the issuing bank is easy to adjust to changing market conditions. For example, if the demand for banknotes would diminish for any reason, the issuing bank would have to reduce its assets and needed flexibility in its portfolio in order to do this. An investment policy concentrating on 'self-liquidating' claims – such as short-term real bills – would then be appropriate for two reasons: first, the bills bought by the bank would be short term and would turn over several times in a year, allowing the volume of lending to be easily adjusted, and second, the business of the debtors would by its 'real' nature generate the cash flow they needed to redeem the bills.

Another argument made for the real bills doctrine was macroeconomic. Smith and many later adherents to the doctrine claimed that if banknotes were covered by real bills only, that would keep their volume in line with the transactions demand for money in the business sector. For Smith, that was important because excessive issue of banknotes could cause liquidity problems for banks when the notes not needed in circulation would return to the bank and presented for cash.

The idea that the real bills doctrine alone could serve as a sufficient guideline for money supply was discredited during the suspension of convertibility of the pound sterling in 1797–1821 when the Bank of England defended its (inflationary) monetary policy by referring to the real bills argument. The Bank of England and its supporters, the antibullionists, ultimately lost the argument to David Ricardo and the 'bullionists', who showed that the increase of the price level (including the prices of gold and foreign exchange) during the suspension of convertibility was evidence of banknotes having been over-issued (see Hollander 1992, Chapter 11). From the modern point of view it is obvious that the real bills doctrine, by itself, leaves the general price level undetermined, and would need to be complemented by something else (the gold standard, or an interest rate rule) to determine the price level (see e.g. Humphrey 1982). It should be noted, however, that this does not invalidate Smith's arguments, which were always presented under the assumption that the monetary system was on a metallic standard.

The scope of application of the real bills doctrine grew as banking developed. Originally, Smith wrote about banks which operated in gold standard conditions, issuing banknotes redeemable with ready money (gold). Although he praised the contemporary lending practices of the Bank of England, he did not make a distinction between private banks of issue and public (central) banks, as this distinction had not fully developed in his time. Later, when modern deposit banking started to grow, the real bills doctrine was applied to several different types of institutions: not only private note-issuing banks but also to central banks of issue (which evolved into central banks) and to commercial banks taking demand deposits from the general public.

The foundation of the Federal Reserve System in 1913 is perhaps the strongest evidence of how strong the influence of the real bills doctrine still was after more than 130 years after *The Wealth of Nations* had been published. According to the act of congress founding it, the task of the US central bank was to provide an 'elastic currency', which would adjust according to the needs of trade, and to 'afford means of rediscounting commercial paper'. The wording follows the real bills doctrine in a clearly recognizable form. It is interesting to note that as the Federal Reserve System was founded under the gold standard, price stability was taken to be guaranteed by the link to gold and was not included in the objectives of the System. However, one of the stated objectives of the System was to make banking supervision more effective.

The Federal Reserve Act of 1913 regulated the lending activities of the Federal Reserve Banks strictly in accordance with the real bills doctrine:

... any Federal Reserve Bank may discount notes, drafts, and bills of exchange arising out of actual commercial transactions; that is, notes, drafts, and bills of exchange issued or drawn for agricultural, industrial, or commercial purposes ... Nothing in this Act contained shall be construed to prohibit such notes, drafts, and bills of exchange, secured by staple agricultural products or other goods, wares, or merchandise from being eligible for such discount; but such definition shall not include notes, drafts, or bills covering merely investments or issued or drawn for the purpose of carrying or trading in stocks, bonds, or other investment securities, except bonds and notes of the Government of the United States. (Federal Reserve Act, Section 13)

The adherence of the Federal Reserve to the real bills doctrine and its reluctance to open market purchases of Government bonds after the 1929 Wall Street crash and in the early years of the Great Depression were later widely condemned. The most influential analysis was by Milton Friedman and Anna Schwartz, who in their classic *Monetary History of the United States* interpret the early part of the Great Depression in the United States as a liquidity crisis and claim that it could easily have been cut short by adopting a different, less restrictive lending policy by the Fed. They also criticize the contemporary academic opinion of thinking that liquidity problems had been solved once and for all by the mere establishment of the Federal Reserve (with its discount window) and did not even recognize the banking collapse that was going on (Friedman and Schwartz 1963, 407–419).

5.3 The Antecedents to the Real Bills Doctrine

To fully understand why the real bills doctrine came into being and what Smith wanted to achieve, it is necessary to understand the context in which he was writing. Smith did not theorize in a vacuum. Instead, his formulation of the real bills doctrine was a reaction to recent events and to some previous literature on banking. Smith's purpose was to argue against certain less restrictive ideas of banking.

He supports his arguments with historical evidence, particularly from Scotland, where banking and banknotes were particularly highly developed already in the eighteenth century and where different kinds of banking models had been tried.

In particular, Smith's statement of the real bills doctrine can be seen as a refutation of the banking principles expounded by his mercantilist contemporary, Sir James Steuart. Although Smith does not mention Steuart by name in *The Wealth of Nations*, he mentioned in his correspondence that the desire to 'confute' the 'fallacious principles' of Steuart was one of the objectives of writing *The Wealth of Nations*.[1]

What were these 'fallacious principles' Smith set out to refute? Steuarts's main work, called *An Inquiry into the Principles of Political Oeconomy* (1767), was written a decade before *The Wealth of Nations*. The book covers many subjects, and banking is one out of many where Steuart's views differ sharply from Smith's. Steuart advocates the establishment of 'banks of circulation based on mortgage'. By monetizing fixed property, these banks could transform it into liquid form, 'melt it down', as Steuart puts it (Steuart 1966, 479–482).

Steuart divides bank credit into three categories: 'private' (backed by some security, real or movable); 'mercantile' (backed by obligations of merchants or manufacturers); and 'public' (based on confidence in a sovereign state). Contrary to what Smith would later propose, Steuart considered mercantile credit, including trade bills, as the most insecure of these, being based on 'opinion and speculation'. For instance, 'the bankruptcy of one considerable merchant may give a shock to mercantile credit all over Europe.' Instead, Steuart argues strongly in favour of more tangible real backing for money – in effect mortgages of land (Steuart 1966, 471–475).

Unlike Smith, Steuart considers liquidity of the collateral to be a secondary consideration only for the rational creditor: 'Coin may be wanting, upon some occasions, to men of the greatest landed property. Is this a reason to suspect their credit?' He considered mortgages on fixed property to be the preferable backing to banknotes because of the greater security and solidity it would give the banking institution (Steuart 1966, 481).

Steuart says that especially in countries where trade and industry are in their infancy, 'it is proper to establish a bank upon the principles

---

[1] Quoted e.g. in Anderson and Tollison (1984).

of private credit. This bank must issue notes upon land and other securities, and the profits of it must arise from the permanent interest drawn from the money lent.' He goes on: 'Of this nature are the banks in Scotland. To them the improvement of this country is entirely owing' (Steuart 1966, 476–477). Steuart was referring to the two big note-issuing banks in the country, the Bank of Scotland and the rival Royal Bank of Scotland, which were accustomed to secured loans and did not concentrate on the discounting of bills (Checkland 1975, 258–260).

Steuart was not the first to recommend the monetization of land. The questions of land banks and of money backed by real property were very topical in the eighteenth century, starting from John Law's 'Money and Trade Considered' (1705), in which he first proposed the 'melting down' of landed property to relieve the prevailing shortage of money, as he saw it.

Smith refers to John Law in *The Wealth of Nations* as a warning example, but his ideas seem to be inspired mainly by the collapse of the Ayr Bank in 1772, an event which occurred after the publication of Steuart's book. Ayr Bank was a short-lived banking company which for awhile dominated the entire note circulation in Scotland. According to Smith, it lent, 'upon any reasonable security', even the full capital required for 'improvements of which the returns are the most slow and distant, such as improvements of land.' As regards discounting of bills, Smith writes that it did not make a distinction between 'real' and 'circulating' bills but discounted all equally. In other words, the activities of the Ayr Bank were exactly those which Smith rejected by his real bills doctrine. The bank eventually collapsed, and Smith concludes that the country suffered a considerable loss by its operations (Smith 1991, 281–282).

Smith knew that there had been a land bank proposal in England in the late seventeenth century, competing with the bill-based alternative of the Bank of England, but it was not adopted, and the operations of the Bank of England developed along the lines of the real bills doctrine (Murphy 1997, 50–51).

Even though contemporary criticism of the real bills doctrine during the suspension of the gold standard in England (by Ricardo, for instance) and in later scholarship (notably Friedman and Schwarz) has presented the doctrine mainly as a fallacious antithesis of the quantity theory, the original purpose of the real bills doctrine seems mainly to have been to oppose the mercantilist idea of land banks. It is clear that both Smith and the later proponents of the real bills doctrine saw the real bills doctrine as a way to safeguard the sustainable liquidity of the banking system, operating under the constraint of a metallic standard.

5.4 A Remark on Narrow, and Central, Banking

The other main ingredient of the classical monetary thought (apart from the real bills doctrine) was the *currency principle*. This is an old idea which became fully articulated in the course of the great monetary policy controversies (the bullionist and currency controversy) in England during the first half of the nineteenth century in the writings of David Ricardo and Lord Overstone.

From the perspective of investment doctrines for banks, the currency controversy of the 1840s can be interpreted as concerning the issue of whether the same principles which had been proposed for private banks would also apply for a central bank, under the conditions of a metallic standard. The currency school of thought, to which both Ricardo and Lord Overstone belonged, claimed that this is not the case. A bank in charge of a nation's circulation should not invest freely even in most liquid bills. According to the proponents of the currency principle, banknotes should be 'representative money' only, and emulate the functioning of purely metallic circulation in most respects, except for the benefits of greater convenience and reduced transaction costs (Daugherty 1942). Closest modern equivalents to the currency principle would be the ideas of narrow banking (as in Friedman 1960) and currency boards (Williamson 1995).

The currency principle had its roots in the rules governing the operation of the ancient public banks of exchange such as the municipal banks of Amsterdam (Amsterdamsche Wisselbank, 1609–1819) and Hamburg (Hamburger Bank, 1619–1875). These so-called *giro banks*, established already in the first decades of the seventeenth century, concentrated on unifying the means of payments in their home cities by providing an account-based alternative to metallic means of payment. They maintained – or at least were supposed to maintain – 100 per cent metallic cover of their liabilities, and a fixed exchange rate between metal (silver) and the account-based money they created, so that they could not influence the quantity of money (van Dillen 1964, 79–160).

In the nineteenth-century debates, the proponents of the currency principle often accepted a fixed 'fiduciary quota' of money which could be covered by assets such as bills of exchange or government bonds. This arrangement preserved, however, the ideal that any changes in the volume of banknotes in circulation would have to reflect corresponding changes in the metallic reserve of the bank of issue.

The idea of 100 per cent cover for banknotes, over and above the possible fiduciary quota, became very widely applied in central banks all over the world. In particular, that was the basis of the Bank of England reform after the Peel Banking Act of 1844 which divided the Bank of England into two departments, one construed as a narrow bank of issue, and the other a lending institution which operated along the lines of the real bills doctrine.

5.5 The Shiftability Doctrine

The real bills doctrine was always an ideal from which actual banking practices deviated to some degree. The British banking system followed the doctrine relatively closely, however, whereas the continental European tradition, where universal banking became common in the latter half of the nineteenth century, was clearly in conflict with the doctrine. In the United States, the deposit banks had always practiced some longer-term lending and investing in securities, even though this was apparently usually considered as an imperfection and a compromise of the ideal state of affairs.

Regarding liquidity policy, it was gradually acknowledged by the early twentieth century that much of banks' liquidity was not in fact based on the maturing of their short-term assets such as bills of exchange, but instead on the possibility of banks to sell some of their investment assets in case of need for cash. It was recognized that bankers were not in fact able to reduce their bill portfolios quickly, since the customers were in practice dependent on rolling over their acceptance credit with the banks. Therefore, other assets had to be relied upon, as cash holdings ('primary reserve') alone were not sufficient to guarantee banks' liquidity in all circumstances. The 1911 edition of Gilbart (1911, pp. 285–300), the classic British banking manual, discussed investments in government securities with emphasis on their liquidity, although England had very conservative banking traditions at the time.

The idea that the liquidity of a bank actually was not based on the maturity of its assets but on its holdings of assets, 'regardless of their nature', which could readily be sold, was labelled as the 'shiftability theory' of liquidity. The idea was the assets could be 'shifted' to other banks or investors when necessary. Moulton (1918) summed up the shiftability doctrine in the dictum 'liquidity is tantamount to shiftability' (Mints 1945, p 265; Moulton 1918).

Mitchell (1923) presented the essence of the shiftability theory in the form of the following points:

- Short-term paper for commercial purposes does not liquidate at maturity.
- Good banking policy would avoid a general forced liquidation of such paper.
- Reliance for the liquidity of earning assets in a crisis must be placed in the ability to shift the earning assets 'to an institution with a stronger cash or credit position'.
- (In crises) banks have reduced their liquid reserves and are less able to meet the demands of depositors immediately.
- The liquidity of assets depends not so much of their maturity or nature but on the institutional organization and coordination of the banking system as a whole.

The first two points on this list constitute a criticism of the real bills doctrine, emphasizing the fact that although credit in the form of discounted bills of exchange was nominally short term, in practice this is not the case, at least not without significant damage to the clientele. To withdraw it would disrupt the business of the debtors and harm the customer relationships. The second two points relate to the observed behaviour of the banks and their use of interbank markets as the primary source of liquidity. The last point relates to the requirements that the use of securities markets as a source of liquidity (as opposed to the self-liquidating nature of short-term assets) puts on the structure of those markets.

Actual developments in the commercial banking sector in the interwar period demonstrated the declining practical importance of the real bills doctrine. In the United States, for instance, the share of rediscountable paper (i.e. bills eligible at the Federal Reserve discount window) in banks' total assets declined from 45 per cent in 1915 to mere 8 per cent in 1935. The share of investment assets (bonds owned plus loans secured by bonds, stocks and real estate) increased correspondingly (Morton 1939). In other countries, the large amounts of government paper which the banks held after the First World War similarly underscored the role of investment securities in banks' liquidity management practices.

The obvious problem with the shiftability theory is the 'fallacy of composition': What is true for a single bank was not necessarily true for the sector as a whole. Although the investment portfolio of a bank might have seemed quite liquid in normal circumstances, when the bank could always find buyers for the bonds it might want to sell, this was not true at the aggregate level. In case the general public tried to withdraw deposits from all banks simultaneously, the banks could not generate additional liquidity by shifting their assets to their peers. In principle, if banks could sell their investment assets to the non-bank sector, they could replenish their cash holdings in that way, but in conditions of general run for liquidity this may not be a realistic option. Then, the remaining source of liquidity is the central bank. This became evident in the 1930s in those countries which experienced a severe financial crisis (including the United States, Germany and some others) and caused important changes in how liquidity was generated and distributed.

The banking crises of the 1930s and the abandonment of the gold standard as a restrictive norm for what monetary policy could do led to changes in the investment and lending policies of the central banks too. They had to become much more pragmatic than before, and in many cases began purchasing long-term securities and government paper in their open market operations. In the United States and the United Kingdom, for example, open market operations eventually became a more important method of monetary control than the traditional method of discounting bills of exchange.

The developments in the United States are an illustrative case. There, the banking crisis of the early 1930s led to changes which distanced the Federal Reserve policy from the real bills doctrine. The Banking Acts of 1933 and 1935 made the collateral policy of the Federal Reserve more flexible than previously, leaving the eligibility of collateral essentially at the discretion of the Board of Governors. These Acts also made open market operations in US government securities a more effective and normal monetary policy instrument by creating the Federal Open Market committee which obtained much greater powers than its predecessor, the Open Market Policy Conference, had (Meltzer 2003, 428–441 and 484–486).

The conditions during the Second World War removed the Federal Reserve policy even further from the practices of the real bills doctrine, as it started to automatically finance the government budget deficits in a large scale and at a fixed rate of interest. Return to more normal practice began only after 1951 (Hetzel and Leach 2001). Although the Federal Reserve thereafter generally sought to keep the maturity of its securities portfolio short, there was no return to the old real bills orthodoxy in terms of investment maturities or in the eligibility requirements applied to collateral acceptable at the discount window.

5.6 After the Great Depression: The Anticipated Income theory

The events of the Great Depression revealed the underlying weaknesses of both the classical real bills doctrine and the interwar shiftability theory. There was a general increase in the demand for liquidity and frequent waves of deposit withdrawals from financially weak banks occurred. It became clear that in a crisis where the public sought to convert their deposits to cash in a large scale, a fatal shortage of liquidity might ensue, and the previous liquidity doctrines could not prevent that from happening.

The kind of collateral that satisfied the requirements of the real bills doctrine would not generate cash quickly enough simply through the bills becoming due. There was the possibility of rediscounting these bills at the central banks' discount window but, in conditions of a general business decline, the supply of commercial bills of exchange was reduced and was not sufficient to prevent a fatal shortage of liquidity. This was the crux of the monetarist critique of the Federal Reserve policy in the early part of the Great Depression in Friedman and Schwartz's (1963) classic analysis. In continental Europe, the situation was even more precarious as banks were heavily involved in long-term lending and other investment, which meant that the bill portfolios were not large relative to the potential deposit outflows.

The shiftability theory of the 1920s did not work well either, since shifting investment assets to other (deposit) banks would not add to aggregate liquidity unless the surplus securities were ultimately purchased and monetized by the central bank. Moreover, under the gold standard even the central banks were reluctant to monetize securities in a large scale for the fear of financing gold outflows which would deplete their reserves.

Lloyd Mints, a prominent banking theorist of the 1940s, expressed the experience of the 1930s with the real bills doctrine and the shift-ability theory as follows (Mints 1945, 263):

The truth is that there is no banking asset which is liquid in the sense that the aggregate amount of this asset can be greatly contracted without dele-terious effects on the volume of output. Only the existence of a central mon-etary agency that is willing and able to increase its holdings of a given asset by large amounts will make that asset liquid for the banking system.

As the result of these developments, there was a radical change in the attitudes towards the relative role of the market and the author-ities, especially in the United States, where the crisis of the 1930s had been particularly severe. The change is apparent in the following quote from Morton (1939):

Liquidity is therefore no longer a 'natural' or 'market' idea but an insti-tutional, legal, or conventional concept. Commercial banking theory is a holdover from the period when banks presumably made only short-term loans and the central bank performed purely banking functions. But it is inadequate under existing circumstances when the central bank is presumed to liquefy actual portfolios and also to use its power to carry out monetary and economic policies.

The 'existing conditions' in the passage refer to the new broader col-lateral policy of the Federal Reserve after the Banking Act of 1935.

After the Great Depression and especially after the Second World War, a new theory of bank lending became prevalent. Even in the United States and the United Kingdom, where banks had previ-ously been reluctant to engage in medium- or long-term lending, attitudes changed and it became accepted to emphasise the general soundness of the potential borrowers more than the liquidity of the loan itself. In continental Europe, where deposit banks had trad-itionally been more involved in long-term lending and even indus-trial ownership, the change was less clear, if at all significant. The term 'anticipated income theory' was coined to describe the newly prevalent doctrine.

The term 'anticipated income' refers to the fact that this doctrine gave up the real bills fiction that the loans would be repaid with the proceeds from the sale of the goods which had been financed by the loan. It was recognised that loans would be repaid from the 'anticipated income' of the customer/borrower which thus became regarded as the real source of bank liquidity.

Herbert Prochnow, the Chicago banker and writer, explained the emergence of the anticipated income theory by several factors, including the following (Prochnow 1949):

• Large excess reserves the banks had after the Second World War (which presumably reduced the weight of the liquidity aspect in bank lending decisions)
• A decline in the demand for short-term commercial loans
• Changes in the discount window policy of the Federal Reserve System, where longer-term assets were now accepted as collateral
• The establishment of the Federal Deposit Insurance system, which reduced the probability of large deposit withdrawals and hence the need for liquid assets
• In terms of managing unexpected liquidity shocks, the reliance of the anticipated income theory on the central bank's liquidity creating powers

It is evident from Prochnow's characterisation of the post-war conditions that liquidity considerations were no longer as prominent as before for the investment doctrines of banks. As a result, profitability of lending and the long-term viability of the borrowers rose to a more prominent role in the banks' lending decisions. This explains the increased willingness of banks at the time to engage in the financing of fixed investment, and also of consumption, activities which would have been quite suspect according to both the real bills doctrine (which preferred short-term bills) and the shiftability doctrine (which preferred marketable securities). It is as if banking was reverting to the pre-Smithian mode where the underlying solvency of the borrower was the most important consideration.

Moreover, it was thought, as noted by Prochnow, that 'the banker has the obligation to work with his customers through good and bad times renewing short-term credit where necessary to assist a borrower who will be able to retire his loan ultimately, but not at the moment'.

So, the liquidity provided by following the real bills doctrine was seen as more or less illusory, and unreliable at best.

The anticipated income theory accepted that the short-term loans which the real bills doctrine had relied on were not in practice always short term or self-liquidating but in fact were often renewed and used to finance longer term capital needs. This realism had also been the basis of the shiftability doctrine, which, however, had proved insufficient without the liquidity guarantees of central banks.

It may be asked what changes occurred in monetary policy corresponding to the adoption of the anticipated income doctrine in commercial banking. The answer seems to be found not in the investment and credit policies of the central banks but in the general tenor of economic policy. The anticipated income doctrine fit well with the post-war Keynesian economics which put the responsibility for the macroeconomic stability in the hands of the fiscal and monetary policy authorities. The origins of the banking problems of the 1930s were seen in macroeconomic instability which could be mitigated with appropriate monetary and fiscal policies. As far as the liquidity of a fundamentally profitable bank depends on macroeconomic stability, the focus on the liquidity of its portfolio would be of secondary importance at best. It was seen as the job of the authorities to provide a stable financial environment for the banks and their customers.

As regards possible liquidity needs which might arise, it is evident from Prochnow's list given earlier that the anticipated income theory relied mainly on the central bank as the provider of liquidity in the last instance. It has a more explicit role here than under the shiftability doctrine. The anticipated income doctrine puts great reliance on the information possessed by the central bank. If the central bank has superior information on the quality of assets of the banks which apply for liquidity, it can potentially solve the liquidity problem which is created by the asymmetry of information among the participants in the private money market.

This exposes a weak point in the doctrine. If the anticipated income theory relies on the liquidity support available at the central bank, it assumes that the central bank is able to monetize good collateral in an efficient way, should the need arise. This is not necessarily the case, as the central bank faces important information problems. The central bank or other supervisory authorities do not in fact have complete information on the value of the assets of the banks. Although central banks are not profit-maximizing agents, they are not indifferent either with respect to the losses which their liquidity support to private banks might ultimately generate.

In addition to the information problem between the central bank and the bank requiring liquidity, there is another at least as difficult information problem between the central bank and its political principals (the government, the legislature, the voters). Even if the central bank itself may be satisfied that the bank asking for liquidity support is ultimately solvent (provided it gets the loan it requests), this may be hard to communicate to the politicians of the general public which are reluctant to risk 'taxpayer money' in rescuing banks in distress.

5.7 Liability Management

One of the most important changes in banking practice in the last half century was the growth of liability management as a doctrine of bank balance sheet management. This went hand in hand with the growth of money markets. Starting from the late 1960s, first in the United States and then in other countries too, large banks started to rely increasingly on their ability to borrow from short-term money markets as a source of liquidity. The following early description contrasts liability management to the previous mainstream of banking theory (Luckett and Steib 1978):

Prior to the 1960s, banking theory was concerned exclusively with the asset side of the bank's balance sheet and the 'menu' of assets deemed appropriate for the bank to acquire. The bank was viewed as a mere passive accepter of liabilities with no control over their size or mix. With the development of such bank-liability instruments as federal funds, negotiable certificates of deposit, and Eurodollars, however, banks moved from passive acceptance of their liabilities to the active management of both sides of the balance sheet.

The description, written from an American perspective, may exaggerate the qualitative change brought about by liability management practices in the 1960s. In Europe, wholesale borrowing by banks had been more prevalent than in the United States even before the Second World War. For instance, the huge capital imports of Germany which occurred after the Dawes stabilization of 1924 took the form of foreign short-term deposits in big German banks, which thus became an important conduit for capital imports (e.g. Aldcroft 1987, 255–257).

The historical examples notwithstanding, the vast growth of the money markets since the 1960s had an epoch-making influence on the financial history of the following decades. Seen after the beginning of this change, the president of the Federal Reserve Bank of Minneapolis, Bruce MacLaury, defined liability management as

a conscious, aggressive use of funds purchased by a bank to supplement deposit growth, thus expanding earning assets and revenues faster than otherwise would be possible. In less pedantic terms: bankers' efforts to go out and get the money any way they can. Obviously, the concept is a matter of degree because bankers from time immemorial have been out beating the bushes for deposits. Buying funds via liability management is merely a different intensity of what has long been a major thrust of bank managers. (MacLaury 1973)

As banks found that they could use the interbank money market as a source of liquidity, the need to hold liquid assets became less obvious. The use of liability management to ensure bank liquidity became a possible and attractive alternative to holding liquid assets.

It is obvious that liability management as a liquidity policy of banks can be seen as an application of the anticipated income theory: a bank practicing liability management expects that it is able to borrow when needed because a prospective lender expects the return on the bank's assets, even if they are long term, to enable it to cover the cost of borrowing with a high degree of certainty. The underlying assumption is that a bank known to be solvent should always be liquid because of its ability to borrow when needed. In well-functioning money markets, it is assumed, the maturity of the bank's cash flows matters little, if their present value is high enough and certain enough so that the risk of insolvency is small.

Modern economics of information give reason to doubt the general validity of this underlying assumption. It is known from the work of Akerlof (1970), for instance, that the presence of severe asymmetric information problems can prevent decentralized markets from functioning properly, and from Diamond and Dybvig (1983) that the liquidity of a basically solvent bank can be endangered by the multiplicity of market equilibria. Because banks are inherently non-transparent, the resulting asymmetric information problem can make their money market liabilities unmarketable if the suspicion of the bank's condition becomes strong enough. As the severity of the asymmetric information problems can change over time, the ability of the money markets to satisfy banks' liquidity needs can vary even if the banks trying to borrow were fundamentally sound in normal liquidity conditions. This makes the liability management strategy potentially fragile.

The regulators soon understood the fragility of liability management as a source of liquidity. Already in 1974, the Fed expressed its concern over the growing reliance on liability management:

To finance their rapid asset expansion, many larger banks, in particular, have turned to heavy reliance on liability management, involving the issuance of market-type deposit certificates and other liabilities to raise whatever added funds are wanted. Such instruments have proved not only highly interest-sensitive but also highly confidence-sensitive in times of stress. Undue banker confidence in their abilities as liability managers has sometimes contributed to the making of excessive loan commitments. Such promises to lend are a practical part of everyday banking, but those promises have not always been prudently limited to amounts that banks could effectively handle in times of strong credit pressures.[2]

In practice, despite these prescient concerns, the markets functioned well enough for the banking industry to become more and more reliant on liability management. The decades of 1980s and 1990s witnessed a dramatic increase in liability management and the use in banking of short-term funds borrowed from money markets.

5.8 The Great Deregulation and the Basel Reforms

The philosophy of banking regulation which was prevalent in the industrialised world after the crises of the Great Depression and the Second World War was to a large extent based on conduct regulation: it concerned what banks were permitted or not permitted to do. The best known example is of course the Glass–Steagall act in the United States, which strictly limited the range of activities deposit

---

[2] Statement of Robert C. Holland before the House Subcommittee on Bank Supervision and Insurance. *Federal Reserve Bulletin* (1974).

banks could engage in. In many European countries, conduct regulation was even more extensive.

In the 1970s the trend in public policy turned from conduct regulation of banks to prudential regulation, where the focus was less on the composition of the banks' asset portfolios and increasingly on capital adequacy. Internationally, this trend was driven by the Basel Committee on banking supervision which was established in 1975 after the collapse of Herstatt Bank and the ensuing credit crunch. The first set of recommendations agreed by the committee, known as the Basel Capital Accord, was published in 1988. It related the capital requirements of banks to the approximate credit risk in the main asset categories. The next generation of the Basel rules, known as Basel II, was released in 2004. It continued the focus on capital adequacy in bank regulation (Goodhart 2011).

The deregulation of bank conduct and the concurrent liberalization of cross-border capital movements were facilitated by the collapse of the international system of fixed exchange rates which happened in the early 1970s. One argument for capital controls had been to protect the foreign currency reserves of central banks from capital flows caused by exchange rate speculation. This argument lost force in countries which floated their currencies. In the context of rapidly internationalizing banks, the conduct regulations previously applied begun to seem outdated and cumbersome. This prepared ground for a new, prudential approach which aimed at just making sure that banks had enough capital to cover the risks they had taken by their lending and investment decisions.

One of the changes which began during the deregulation of the 1980s and turned to have momentous effects in the financial crisis of the 2000s was the spread of securitization. This is a financial strategy closely related to the old shiftability doctrine, however, with the difference that in securitization the assets are meant to be sold right away, instead of being kept as a 'secondary liquidity reserve' and sold only if liquidity is needed.

In normal conditions, securitisation and selling of some assets of a bank would seem to reduce liquidity risk as the funding needs are transferred to the purchaser of the securitized assets. However, when used as a business model, securitization makes the bank more reliant on the functioning and stability of financial markets. During times of financial market stress the bank may have to postpone planned sales and warehouse the assets in question, with the financing requirements that such warehousing entails.

Some forms of securitization may also give rise to contingent liquidity risk, i.e. the possibility that the bank will be called upon to provide liquidity unexpectedly in the market of securitized assets, potentially at a time when it is already under stress (BIS 2008).

Regarding the choice of business models of banks, the decades of the 1990s and the early 2000s saw further deregulation of bank conduct and of bank portfolios. In the United States, the Gramm–Leach–Bliley Act of 1999 effectively repealed the Glass–Steagall Act, which had separated investment banking from deposit banking since the 1930s.

The transition to floating exchange rates also changed the conditions under which central banks operated. Basically, the liquidity concerns of the central banks issuing a floating currency were dramatically reduced. Under the system of floating exchange rates, the liquidity requirements of modern central banks are clearly different from those of the deposit banks. As issuers of legal tender, and in the absence of an obligation to exchange their liabilities to gold or to foreign currency at some given exchange rate, the ability of the central banks to discharge their debt obligations is not in doubt.[3] On the other hand, the increased volume of international capital flows posed new and even more challenging demands on the international liquidity of those central banks which continued to follow a fixed exchange rate strategy (Johnson-Calari, Grava and Kobor 2007).

5.9 The Great Financial Crisis and Its Aftermath

Despite a number of country-specific or regional liquidity crises, mostly in emerging markets,[4] the interbank money markets worked well enough until the first decade of the 2000s for the banking industry to become increasingly reliant on liability management for its liquidity.

---

[3] In the case of central banks operating under a floating exchange rate, the question of their liquidity takes another form: whether, in the case of a sudden decrease in the demand for central bank money, the central bank is able to reduce the supply of money in the same degree, lest the decrease in the demand for central bank money will show up as a decrease in its value.

[4] The Latin American Crisis of 1982 and the Asian Crisis of 1997 should be mentioned here since they occurred after periods of particularly large-scale interbank short-term borrowing from the international markets by the affected countries.

The global financial crisis which culminated in 2008 was an enormous shock to the contemporary liquidity management practices, however. As a result, the liability management strategy which had dominated the deregulation era has been largely discredited after the financial crisis. The interbank money markets which the banks had come to rely on dried up as the result of the uncertainty (asymmetric information) of the participating banks' financial health after the subprime crisis. The fragilities and the mechanism of sudden illiquidity had been lucidly described by Raghuram Rajan already before the crisis erupted (Rajan 2005).

While there are different views of the ultimate causes of the crisis, it is generally recognized that it was triggered by a decline in the prices of US residential real estate which had been used as collateral in asset-backed securities in a large scale. The combination of real estate collateral with short-term funding has been identified as a central ingredient in the events (e.g. Holmström and Tirole 2011, 230–241). The liquidity in the securitized mortgage bond markets was sharply reduced during the crisis and this phenomenon spread also to other bond markets, with the exception of some most highly regarded sovereign bonds such as German bunds and the US treasuries. Consequently, the modern version of the shiftability doctrine, which had been manifested in the belief that bond portfolios were reliably liquid not only in benign conditions but always, was at least temporarily refuted.

As a result of these events, the crisis caused a sharp change in the hitherto prevailing attitude towards banks' business models and banking regulation. It was realized that the emphasis on solvency and collateral had been too uncritical and the theoretically much more thorny liquidity issues had to be taken seriously both by regulators and by the banks themselves.

The regulatory response has been clearly visible in the work of the Basel Committee on Bank supervision, which has recently given liquidity a much greater role than before in its regulatory agenda. Consequently, a number of regulatory changes have been proposed after the financial crisis and are being implemented more or less in line with the Basel Committee recommendations. Two such changes which pertain directly to liquidity management of banks are the introduction of the Liquidity Coverage Ratio (LCR) requirement and the requirement for a Net Stable Funding Ratio (NSFR). The former requires that the bank should have in its possession enough high-quality liquid assets to meet its liquidity needs for 30 days in a scenario of a severe liquidity outflow. The latter requirement stipulates, roughly speaking, that the bank's illiquid assets must be financed with long-term liabilities so that the bank would not get into trouble in case its deposit base would be depleted for some reason.[5]

Viewed in the context of the historical bank investment doctrines, the LCR strongly resembles the shiftability doctrine, which relied on the ability of the bank to sell some of its assets should it get short of cash. The parallel between the LCR and the shiftability doctrine is highlighted by the observation that in the LCR, the eligible high-quality liquid assets are not typically limited to those with a short maturity (see BIS 2013, 2014).

The NSFR, for its part, has some resemblance to the real bills doctrine as it seeks to match the liability structure of the assets and liabilities to some extent, and limits the extent to which a bank which mainly has liquid liabilities can invest in illiquid assets. On the other hand, the way the NSFR is calculated shows the influence of the shiftability doctrine as even long securities are treated as liquid if they have low credit risk and are traded in 'large, deep and active' markets (BIS 2013).

As the Bank for International Settlements (BIS) recommendations are being implemented in the most important jurisdictions in the world, albeit with some local modifications, we can conclude that in the regulators' sphere, the crisis has indeed brought liquidity issues back to focus but they have not resurrected the real bills doctrine. Rather, the regulatory initiatives are close to the shiftability doctrine with its reliance on markets and the ability to monetize some assets by selling them to other investors.

Even more dramatic than the response of the regulators has been the change in the liquidity behaviour of banks. The banks – especially in Europe but also in the United States – accumulated unprecedented amounts of free reserves in their accounts at the central bank. This partly could be due to the decreased opportunity cost of holding reserves as central bank lending rates have decreased close to zero after the crisis of 2008. However, there is also evidence that a precautionary

---

[5] Different asset and liability categories are accounted for with different 'Available Stable Funding (ASF)' and 'Required Stable Funding (RSF)' factors when the net stable funding ratio is calculated (BIS 2014).

motive has been at work in the large-scale reserve hoarding by banks. This is in sharp contrast to the previously prevalent liability management strategy of the pre-crisis era (Berrospide 2013).

A similar shift towards an emphasis on precautionary hoarding of liquidity can be observed in the behaviour of central banks. The amount of foreign exchange reserves held by central banks across the world has increased dramatically in the last fifteen years. The experiences of financial crises are a natural explanation of this trend, but it seems that in the emerging economies, this reserve accumulation started already after the Asian crisis of 1997 rather than the international financial crisis of 2008 (IMF 2010). In any case, also the central banks (at least in the emerging market economies) have clearly revised their priorities in favour of accumulating more international liquidity.

5.10 Conclusions

The historical development of the banking doctrines has mostly revolved around the question of liquidity. The review of the history of ideas in banking reveals that this is a recurring debate which has been going on for almost 250 years and is still unresolved. Of course, each generation of economists and bankers has approached the problems from its particular point of view which is determined by the problems of the time.

The real bills doctrine arose as a response to the instability of banks experienced in the eighteenth century when the modern banking ideas were just emerging. As a restrictive business principle, the real bills doctrine was naturally prone to being watered down over time whenever strong evidence which would have reminded banks of its underlying rationale was not forthcoming. The real bills doctrine may also have hindered financial development by its insistence of very short-term nature of bank lending. In any case, the shiftability doctrine which gradually supplanted the real bills doctrine in commercial banking was decidedly less demanding in terms of banks' reliance in their own liquidity and more reliant on the ability of markets to provide liquidity when needed. At the same time, it facilitated more long-term financing by the banks.

The Great Depression was followed by a period, beginning in the 1940s, when the liquidity of banking assets seemed a secondary concern. Perhaps paradoxically, this period included both the years of

Keynesianism, when macroeconomic policy and accommodative monetary policies of central banks reduced the banks' need to worry about
their liquidity, and the intellectually very different years of deregulation, when the faith in the ability of financial markets to solve liquidity problems reached its high point. In any case, the decades from the
1940s until the financial crisis of the first decade of the 2000s witnessed a shift from asset-based liquidity management to other methods, increasingly relying on liability management.

This trend was in tune with the assumption of perfect markets
which was very popular in financial research in the 1980s and the
1990s. Although the economics of asymmetric information discovered
the adverse effects of asymmetric information already in the 1970s
and early 1980s, practitioners (both the regulators and the bankers)
seemed often to work on the simpler and more benign assumption that
solvency ensures liquidity.

The crisis that began in 2007 has brought about a very significant
reassessment of the question of liquidity of the bank portfolios. Today's
regulatory agenda and the banks' strategic objectives seem to be influenced by two considerations in particular: the desire to prevent the
problems encountered during the last financial crisis from recurring. At
the same time, it has forced the economists and bankers alike to take
seriously the fact that solvency does not guarantee liquidity but must
be taken separately into consideration. Perhaps the current thinking
about bank liquidity and its role in the investment doctrines of banks
is somehow approaching the ideas of Adam Smith and his followers.

References

Akerlof, G. A. (1970). The Market for "Lemons": Quality Uncertainty and
    the Market Mechanism. *The Quarterly Journal of Economics*, 84:3,
    488–500.
Aldcroft, D. H. (1987). *From Versailles to Wall Street*. Aylesbury: Pelican Books.
Anderson, G. and Tollison, R. (1984). Sir James Steuart as the Apotheosis
    of Mercantilism and His Relation to Adam Smith. *Southern Economic
    Journal*, 51:2, 456–468.
Berrospide, J. (2013): *Bank Liquidity Hoarding and the Financial Crisis: An
    Empirical Evaluation*. Washington, DC: Finance and Economics
    Discussion Series Divisions of Research & Statistics and Monetary
    Affairs Federal Reserve Board.

BIS (2008). *Principles for Sound Liquidity Risk Management and Supervision*. Basel Committee on Banking Supervision. Basel: Bank for international Settlements.

BIS (2013). *Basel III: The Liquidity Coverage Ratio and Liquidity Risk Monitoring Tools*. Basel Committee on Banking Supervision. Basel: Bank for International Settlements.

BIS (2014). *Basel III: The Net Stable Funding Ratio*. Basel Committee on Banking Supervision. Basel: Bank for International Settlements.

Checkland, S. G. (1975). *Scottish Banking. A History, 1695–1973*. Glasgow: Collins.

Daugherty, M. (1942). The Currency-Banking Controversy. *Southern Economic Journal*, 9:2, 140–155.

Diamond, D. W. and P. H. Dybvig (1983). Bank Runs, Deposit Insurance, and Liquidity. *Journal of Political Economy*, 91:3, 401–419.

Friedman, M. (1960). *A Program for Monetary Stability*. New York: Fordham University Press.

Friedman, M. and Schwartz, A. (1963). *A Monetary History of the United States*. Princeton, NJ: Princeton University Press.

Gilbart, J.W. (1911). *The History, Principles and Practice of Banking*. London: G. Bell and Sons.

Goodhart, C. (1988). *The Evolution of Central Banks*. Cambridge, MA: MIT Press.

(2011). *The Basel Committee on Banking Supervision: A History of the Early Years 1974–1997*. Cambridge: Cambridge University Press.

Hamilton, H. (1956). The Failure of the Ayr Bank, 1772. *The Economic History Review*, New Series, 8:3, 405–417.

Hetzel, R. and Leach, R. (2001). The Treasury-Fed Accord: A New Narrative Account. *The Federal Reserve Bank of Richmond Economic Quarterly*, 87:1, 33–55.

Holland, R. C. (1974). Statement before the Subcommittee on Bank Supervision and Insurance of the Committee on Banking and Currency, U.S. House of Representatives, December 12, 1974. *Federal Reserve Bulletin*, 60, 12.

Hollander, S. (1992). *Classical Economics*. Toronto: University of Toronto Press.

Holmström, B. and Tirole, J. (2011). *Inside and Outside Liquidity*. Cambridge, MA: MIT Press.

Humphrey, T. (1982). The Real Bills Doctrine. *The Federal Reserve Bank of Richmond Economic Quarterly*, 68:3.

IMF (2010). Reserve Accumulation and International Monetary Stability. Paper prepared by the Strategy, Policy and Review Department. Washington, DC: International Monetary Fund.

Johnson-Calari, J., Grava, R. and Kobor, A. (2007). Trends in Reserve Management by Central banks. In A. F. P. Bakker and I. R. Y. van Herpt (eds.) *Central Bank Reserve Management. New Trends from Liquidity to Return.* Cheltenham: Edward Elgar.

Luckett, D. G. and S. B. Steib (1978). Bank Soundness and Liability Management. *Nebraska Journal of Economics and Business*, 17:3, 37–47.

MacLaury, B. K. (1973). Liability Management. Speech December 7, 1973. *Statements and Speeches of Bruce K. MacLaury.* 1971–1976, https:// fraser.stlouisfed.org/title/1114 (Accessed on December 9, 2016).

Meltzer (2003). *A History of the Federal Reserve*, Vol. I: *1913–1951.* Chicago: University of Chicago Press.

Mints, L. (1945). *A History of Banking Theory in Great Britain and the United States.* Chicago: University of Chicago Press.

Mitchell, W. F. (1923). The Institutional Basis for the Shiftability Theory of Bank Liquidity. *The University Journal of Business*, 1:3, 334–356.

Morton, W. A. (1939). Liquidity and Solvency. *American Economic Review*, 29:2, 272–285.

Moulton, H.G. (1918). Commercial Banking and Capital Formation III. *Journal of Political Economy*, 26:7, 484–508.

Murphy, A.E. (1997). *John Law, Economic Theorist and Policy-Maker.* Oxford: Oxford University Press.

Prochnow, H. (1949). Bank Liquidity and the New Doctrine of Anticipated Income. *The Journal of Finance*, 4:4, 298–314.

Rajan, R. (2005). Has Finance Made the World Riskier? In *The Greenspan Era: Lessons for the Future.* Federal Reserve Bank of Kansas City.

Smith, A. (1991). *The Wealth of Nations.* Everyman edition (original 1776).

Steuart, Sir James (1966). *An Inquiry into the Principles of Political Oeconomy,* Vol. Two (original 1765). Chicago: The University of Chicago Press.

Van Dillen, J. G. (1964): *History of Public Banks* (original 1934). London: Frank Cass.

Williamson, J. (1995). *What Role for Currency Boards?* Washington, DC: Institute for International Economics.

6 | Stress Testing in Banking: A Critical Review

ADRIAN POP

6.1 Introduction

Stress testing is used both by banks and other financial institutions in risk management and by prudential authorities in macroprudential regulation, in order to determine how certain extreme, but still plausible, shock scenarios would affect the value of a given asset portfolio or the stability of the financial system as a whole. Before the inception of the global financial crisis during the summer of 2007, the stress tests had been conducted following a *bottom-up* approach, that is, on a bank-by-bank basis. Since then, many observers have advocated for a more extensive use of stress tests, especially as a useful *macroprudential* tool.

From a macroprudential perspective, the main objectives of a stress testing exercise are to properly identify the risk drivers and vulnerabilities that are most likely to generate financial instability and assess the resilience of the banking system to various macroeconomic or financial shocks. Particularly, they allow supervisors to identify the relevant transmission channels of extreme, but still plausible, events affecting the stability of the banking system.

Historically, the Basel Committee on Banking Supervision in its market risk amendment to the first Basel capital accord (Basel I) published in 1996 contains the first references to stress testing (see Basel Committee on Banking Supervision 1996, 46 et passim). Precisely, the supervisory approval to use internal models in order to set capital charges for market risks is granted only to banks that run rigorous and comprehensive stress tests on a regular basis. The several examples of stress scenarios mentioned in the 1996 amendment to the first Basel

Without implicating them in any way, we are grateful to Esa Jokivuolle,
Radu Tunaru, and participants at the University of Kent and Bank of Finland
Conference "From the Last Financial Crisis to the Next," for useful comments
and suggestions. All remaining errors are our own responsibility.

capital accord are all based on past episodes of market turbulence, such as the October 1987 stock market crash; the Exchange Rate Mechanism crisis of 1992–1993; or the bond market crashes observed at the beginning of 1994.

Since the early 1990s, stress testing exercises have been regularly conducted in central banks and supervisory authorities, as well as in the vast majority of internationally active banks and financial institutions. The Basel II capital accord that entered into force at the beginning of 2007 formally asked bank managers to carry out regular stress tests under the Pillar 1 guidelines for internal model validation purposes (see Basel Committee on Banking Supervision, 2006, §434–435). Moreover, Basel II also refers to stress tests under the supervisory approach in Pillar 2 by highlighting that banks should consider the results of such tests in their capital planning process (see Basel Committee on Banking Supervision, 2006, §726).

The topic of stress testing in banking has received renewed attention and has been vividly debated since the inception of the global financial crisis in the summer 2007. For instance, in the United States, the Federal Reserve decided on May 2009 to disclose the results of stress tests conducted by the nineteen major bank holding companies in the country (Supervisory Capital Assessment Program, SCAP). The SCAP evolved into two distinct but related supervisory stress testing programs: (1) the Dodd–Frank Act stress test requirements and (2) the so-called Comprehensive Capital Analysis and Review (CCAR), both conducted on an annual basis.

In the same vein, the European authorities followed the United States in carrying out the first European Union–wide stress tests by September 2009. Earlier European Union–wide stress tests had also been conducted in 2010 (by the Committee of European Banking Supervisors, CEBS), 2011 and 2014 (by the European Banking Authority, EBA). The main features of the European stress scenario, common to all participating banks, were calibrated by the European Central Bank, but the final stress scenario imposed to banks was adapted at the national level by each supervisory authority.

Critics and observers in the financial media argued that the United States and European stress scenarios were too mild to generate credible results. In the United States, for instance, at the end of the first quarter of 2009, actual data on the considered stressed variables, i.e. Gross Domestic Product (GDP) growth, unemployment rate, and home prices, were already *worse* than the adverse scenario proposed for 2010. In Europe, analysts expressed concerns that the earlier stress scenarios were underestimating the potential losses on banks' trading portfolios from depreciations of sovereign (particularly Spanish and Greek) bonds.

By taking a more fundamental, macroprudential, perspective, Borio, Drehmann, and Tsatsaronis (2014) critically reviewed the state of the art in macro stress testing and conclude that stress tests failed at the very junctures when regulators needed them. In their opinion, (macro) stress tests are a useful tool for crisis management and resolution, but are unreliable as an early-warning device during tranquil periods of time, when risks are quietly building up. According to Drehmann, Borio, and Tsatsaronis (2012), the most severe financial crises tend to start developing far before the bust phase, around the peaks of medium-term financial cycles.

Clearly, the reliability and usefulness of the stress test results largely depend on the assumptions backing the stress scenario, as well as on the methodology used to link the risk factors to the financial strength indicators. A study on sound stress testing practices published by the Basel Committee in January 2009 sums up several deficiencies inherent in stress testing exercises conducted by the largest banks and their supervisory authorities before and during the global financial crisis (see BCBS 2009). Among the main culprits are a lack of integration of stress tests into the broad risk governance process; the limitations resulted from disregarding or underestimating specific risks (e.g. securitization-related risks); the failure to take into account second-round effects; and the deficiencies in the design of stress scenarios.[1]

In light of these weaknesses, the aim of the present chapter is to contribute to the growing economic literature on stress testing in banking by focusing on a key methodological issue: the design and calibration of initial shocks to be used in stress scenarios. Although our analysis mainly concerns "macro" stress testing, the basic approach presented here is also applicable to sensitivity analyses and stress tests performed at a bank level.

---

[1] See FSA (2006) and Haldane (2009) for a criticism of the calibration of stress scenarios by the vast majority of UK financial firms before and during the recent financial crisis.

We present and discuss a rigorous and flexible methodological framework to select initial shocks based on statistical techniques conceived to detect outliers and structural breaks in financial and (macro)economic time series. We believe our framework is relevant to the current debate around the appropriate methodology to generate "extreme, but plausible" shocks and stress scenarios. Indeed, the severity of the shock assumed at the beginning of the stress period and the appropriate length of the stress period largely determine the quality of the outcome. For instance, setting the magnitude of the initial shock too high or, more often, too low would undermine either the credibility or the meaning of the whole stress testing exercise.[2] In the same vein, choosing a too narrow or a too wide window for the stress period would either not be sufficient for risk factors to fully materialize or not be compatible with the usual assumptions that banks do not reallocate their portfolios during the whole stress period (see, e.g. De Bandt and Oung 2004). As pointed out by Drehmann (2008), there seems to be no golden rule for the optimal horizon to consider in stress testing. However, according to Isogai (2009) and Sorge (2004), there is a stringent need to apply "objective criteria" in calibrating stress scenarios and to take into account these criteria during the implementation phase.

The chapter is organized as follows. Section 6.2 focuses on some theoretical underpinnings of the various stress testing methodologies in use. We put emphasis on the central role the design of shock scenarios plays in conducting a robust stress testing exercise and discuss the relevant literature containing conceptual, as well as methodological, contributions. Section 6.3 summarizes a novel conceptual and methodological framework that helps to inform the calibration of initial shocks to be used in stress scenarios. We propose a simple numerical example that allows us to illustrate the relevance of the proposed methodology and to highlight some practical implementation issues in Section 6.4. Finally, Section 6.5 concludes.

6.2 Calibration of Stress Scenarios: Guidance from the Literature

There is a vast emerging literature analyzing the various challenging issues, both methodological and practical, of a stress testing exercise.

---

[2] For more details on the credibility issue in stress testing, see Sorge (2004).

Given the aim of the present chapter, we decided to focus our survey of the literature on the role the calibration of shock scenarios plays in conducting a robust and effective stress testing exercise. First, we begin by briefly discussing some relevant conceptual papers. Second, we review several related methodological contributions to this literature. Third, we discuss two methodological issues related to the calibration of the stress scenarios that have the potential to undermine the effectiveness of a stress testing exercise if not taken properly into account.

Among the first methodological surveys, Foglia (2009) proposes an extensive review of the practice of stress testing in use at major central banks and supervisory authorities. Although the focus of her survey is on a particular type of banking risk – the credit risk viewed from a macroeconomic perspective – it reveals, however, a lot of heterogeneity among the methodological approaches embraced by various prudential authorities. The same degree of heterogeneity in stress testing practices has also been noticed in the surveys conducted by the Committee on the Global Financial System (CGFS) in 2000, 2001, and 2005, respectively, at a microeconomic level, i.e. at the bank level. It is, however, worth noting that whatever the adopted methodology is, the implementation of a stress testing exercise takes place in several common steps (for more details, see Sorge 2004; Bunn, Cunningham, and Drehmann 2005; Drehmann 2009; Borio et al. 2014):

• The selection of an initial shock or a combination of initial shocks
• The assessment of the impact of the simulated shock on the macroeconomic environment
• The quantification of the effect of the shock on the probability of default of borrowers and asset prices in general
• The quantification of the induced effect of the stress scenario on the bank profitability and solvency and the macrofinancial stability
• Eventually, the estimation of "feedback" (also called "second round") effects between the financial (or banking) sector and the real economy[3]

As far as the first stage is concerned, Borio et al. (2014) correctly point out that the literature does not make a clear distinction between "shocks" and "scenarios." For some authors, the term "scenario"

---

[3] Only a few recent models take into account this fifth stage. The literature on macro feedbacks in stress testing is scarce (see, e.g. Jokivuolle, Virén, and Vähämaa 2010, which is a notable exception).

describes a set of exogenous shocks, while for others the same term designates both the set of exogenous shocks and their estimated, model-derived, impact on the macroeconomic environment. Generally speaking, in the first stage, the initial shocks are calibrated using either hypothetical scenarios based on experts' opinions and the economic expertise of staff or historical data.[4]

Table 6.1 synthesizes the main advantages and drawbacks of each of the two approaches used to select stress scenarios, while Table 6.2 provides several examples of stress scenarios in use at major financial institutions. The so-called "hypothetical" scenarios are useful when the aim of the stress testing exercise is to assess the impact of shocks related to *innovative* risk factors and *new* financial products for which sufficiently long time-series are rarely, or simply not, available. To give an illustration, the financial crisis that began in 2007 has revealed a worried lack of imagination among senior managers that led to an underestimation of the impact of low-probability events because of cognitive biases and a "false sense of security" (see BCBS 2009; Borio and Drehmann 2009). Hence, it is not by chance that the Basel Committee strongly recommends that stress testing programs should include a large spectrum of hypothetical shocks and scenarios in order to scrutinize new emerging risk drivers related to innovative financial products that are impossible to replicate from previous crisis episodes. Hypothetical shocks are by their very nature forward-looking and help to address this concern. Another advantage of hypothetical, as opposed to historically based, shocks and stress scenarios is that they may be tailored to the risk profile and specific composition of the bank asset portfolio. The most common examples of hypothetical scenarios in macro stress testing of system-wide credit risk are based on large movements in economic growth prospects, e.g., unexpected slowing of the global demand; rises in interest rates and oil prices; a widening of sovereign credit spreads; a severe decline in stock prices; geopolitical tensions or terrorist attacks (see Table 6.2 and CGFS 2005 for a survey).

The most serious drawback of hypothetical scenarios is that they may lack credibility and are hence relatively easy to dismiss by senior managers as implausible. Indeed, as there is no objective rule or guidance

---

[4] The taxonomy of stress scenarios is discussed at length in several related conceptual papers. See, e.g., Blashke et al. (2001); Cihak (2004, 2007); Sorge (2004); CGFS (2005); Drehmann (2008, 2009); Isogai (2009); and more recently, Schuermann (2014).

Table 6.1 *Historical versus hypothetical stress scenarios*

Historically based scenarios	Hypothetical scenarios
Rigorous and objective, less discretionary, transparent, based on clear selection criteria.	Ad hoc, arbitrary, subjective, discretionary, opaque, subject to manipulation because no strict criteria apply for scenario selection.
Objective guidance based on past data.	No rule or guidance in setting the magnitude or the persistence of the initial shock.
Backward-looking by definition.	Forward-looking by nature.
Hard to dismiss by managers as implausible, increased acceptance.	Easy to dismiss by senior managers as implausible.
Credible, plausible, intuitively possible because the extreme movements actually occurred in the past.	Less credible, less plausible, may include unimaginable events.
Underestimation of the severity of the shock in the case of innovative risk factors and new products for which sufficiently long time-series are rarely available.	Based on experts' opinions and the economic expertise of staff, which may underestimate the impact of low-probability events (cognitive bias).
Underestimate the possibility that statistical patterns may break down differently in the future.	A "failure of imagination" that may lead to a false sense of security.
Not necessarily worst-case scenarios.	May include worst-case scenarios.
The composition and risk profile of the bank portfolio are taken into account only when selecting the risk factors.	The composition and risk profile of the bank portfolio may be considered.
Computational-intensive, but likely to be fully automated.	Labor-intensive, more judgment involved.
Based on parametric assumptions and on the assumption that future crises resemble past crises.	
Do not include the possibility of events not previously experienced.	

Source: The author, based on various references discussed in the review of the literature section.

Table 6.2 *Examples of historical and hypothetical stress scenarios in use at major banks*

Historically based scenarios	Hypothetical scenarios
Interest rates	
1994 bond market sell-off	US economic outlook
1997 Asian financial crisis	Global economic outlook
1998 LTCM, Russia	Increase in inflation expectations
2001 09/11 terrorist attacks	
Equities	
1987 Black Monday	Geopolitical unrest
1997 Asian financial crisis	Terrorist attacks
2000 bursting of IT bubble	Global economic outlook
2001 09/11 terrorist attacks	
Foreign exchange	
1992 ERM crisis	Collapse of currency pegs
1997 Asian financial crisis	
1998 Russia	
Commodities	
	Oil price scenario
	Geopolitical unrest in the Middle East
Credit	
1997 Asian financial crisis	Emerging markets economic outlook
1998 Russia	Euro area economic outlook
2001 09/11 terrorist attacks	Global economic outlook
	Natural disasters
	US government-sponsored enterprises
	Terrorist attack
Property	
	Fewer than three per hypothetical episode
Other	
	Bank funding
	Global economy

Note: This table is based on the last (January 2005) survey on stress testing practices conducted by the Committee on the Global Financial System (CGFS, 2005), covering 64 banking organizations and other global financial players headquartered in 16 different countries.

in setting the magnitude or the persistence of shocks in hypothetical scenarios, which may sometimes include "unimaginable" events, they tend to be less credible and plausible than historically based scenarios.

By contrast, historical shocks tend to be based on more rigorous selection criteria and objective guidance grounded on past data. Consequently, they are harder to dismiss by senior managers as implausible and get relatively more acceptance. They are also more credible and plausible than hypothetical shocks and are intuitively possible because the considered extreme movements in risk factors actually occurred at some point of time in the past. The main drawback of historically based shocks and scenarios is that they are generally based on some parametric assumptions that may not be valid under stress conditions and especially on the assumption that future crises are somewhat similar to past crises. They may also lead to an underestimation of the impact in the particular case of innovative risk factors and new emerging financial products for which sufficiently long time-series are, de facto, not available.[5] The vast majority of historical stress scenarios focus on a number of major turbulence episodes observed in the past: the 9/11 terrorist attacks on the United States; the "Black Monday" 1987 stock market crash; the 1998 market turmoil due to the Long-Term Capital Management (LTCM) collapse and the Russian debt default; the 1997 Asian crisis (see Table 6.2).

Our brief description of the main advantages and drawbacks associated to historical and hypothetical shocks and scenarios suggests that important complementarities may (and should) exist between these two main approaches commonly used in the practice of stress testing.

There are a few methodological papers that examine the design of stress scenarios using statistical approaches. As far as the macro-stress testing exercises are concerned, the "stressed" variables within a consistent scenario might be calibrated using structural econometric models or vector autoregressive/error-correction (VAR/VECM) models estimated by central banks for forecasting and monetary policy purposes.[6] An alternative statistical based approach to the calibration of stress scenarios is proposed by Boss et al. (2006) within the Systemic Risk

---

[5] For instance, standard historical scenarios were not able to replicate extremely large movements in risk drivers, such as those observed in the fast-growing Credit Default Swap (CDS) market during the subprime crisis.

[6] These macroeconometric models are extensively reviewed in Foglia (2009). Consequently, they are not discussed in this chapter. Rather, in what follows, we

Monitor (SRM) tool developed at the Oesterreichische Nationalbank.[7] Basically, stress scenarios are simulated by drawing randomly vectors of risk factor changes from a multivariate distribution constructed in two steps. First, marginal risk factor distributions are inferred based on univariate statistical tests that identify, for each relevant risk factor, an empirical model exhibiting the best out-of-sample performance. Second, the correlation structure of the risk factors is modeled by fitting a multivariate *t*-copula to the past data.[8]

The trade-off between plausibility and severity in calibrating stress scenarios is addressed explicitly by Breuer et al. (2009) within a one-period quantitative risk-management framework. They propose a measure of plausibility based on the so-called *Mahalanobis* radius, i.e., the number of standard deviations of the multivariate move from the center of mass characterizing the distribution of the *systematic* risk factors to the stress test point. After retaining all scenarios above a minimum plausibility threshold level, the stress scenarios are identified by performing a systematic worst-case search over the given plausible admissibility domain. This framework has clear advantages over the traditional "hand-picked" approach to select stress scenarios: e.g., no harmful scenarios are missed; no implausible scenarios are retained; and stress scenarios are portfolio specific. However, as noted by Isogai (2009) and Breuer and Csiszár (2013), the approach is applicable only to a family of elliptical (including the normal and

focus our literature review on empirical studies that propose purely statistical approaches, more in line with the aim of the present chapter.

[7] The link between systemic risk and the stress test impact is also studied by Homar, Kick, and Salleo (Chapter 7). They compare two distinct measures of the impact in terms of stress, namely the SRISK measure first proposed by V. Acharya and S. Steffen and the results of the 2014 ECB/EBA stress test. Homar et al. (Chapter 7) explain the discrepancies between the two measures by regressing them on a large set of explanatory factors usually associated with bank credit losses and financial vulnerability (macroeconomic variables, bank balance-sheet variables, and market-based risk factors). While the ECB/EBA stress impact seems to be strongly related with these factors, the SRISK measure is much less explained by the same factors, being driven mainly by the bank's leverage ratio. These discrepancies are due to the fundamental differences in the construction of the two measures of stress.

[8] While the statistical approach described in Boss et al. (2006) presents a certain number of advantages (e.g., explicit modeling of the joint behavior of the stressed variables and of the dependency structure), Foglia (2009) expressed some doubts that it is highly suitable for storytelling and communication purposes.

t-Student) distributions of risk factors and thus may not be suitable for non-elliptically distributed risk factors.

The statistical approach of Breuer et al. (2009) was extended by Breuer et al. (2012) to a multiperiod setting, in which stress scenarios are defined as paths (and not point-in-time values) of macroeconomic variables. Breuer et al. (2012) convincingly show the practical relevance of their approach. Compared with the stress testing results obtained by using traditional approaches, calibrated on real data prior to the subprime crisis, the worst-case scenario comes much nearer to the severity of the economic downturn observed since 2008.[9]

In a related contribution, Varotto (2012) focuses on the role played by the length of the stress period in shaping the stress test results. Basically, he estimates expected credit losses for individual exposures and representative bank portfolios under the most severe default scenario recorded in history: the Great Depression scenario. The worst-case capital based on this extreme scenario is shown to be highly sensitive to the stress horizon. Specifically, by expanding the stress period from one year to three years, he reveals that the worst case capital increases more than three times. Consequently, over a longer (e.g., three-year) stress horizon, banks having low-quality portfolios would not be able to limit losses within their Basel II required minimum.

By considering a purely statistical approach, Dubecq and Gourieroux (2012) propose an interesting distinction between shocks on variables and shocks on distributions within a theoretical framework that allows examining the formal link between the two types of shocks. They illustrate the relevance of this distinction by applying a stress methodology to a portfolio of European sovereign bonds held by a financial institution. The methodology consists of first identifying a Eurozone systematic factor using a standard principal components analysis. Then, the distribution of the systematic factor before the financial crisis of 2007 is considered to set up the so-called "baseline" scenario, while the distribution over the crisis period is interpreted as the "contaminating" distribution (stress scenario). They focus their

---

[9] The traditional approaches considered in Breuer et al. (2012) are a synthetic one-step scenario, in which GDP growth decreases by three standard deviations in the first quarter and then reverts to its long-term path, and a historical recession scenario (the 1992 recession in Spain). The worst-case scenario is calibrated by applying the original methodology proposed by the authors on Spanish data up to December 2006.

analysis on the effects of the stress scenario viewed as a "contamin-
ation" of the Eurozone systematic risk factor on both crystallized and
optimally updated portfolios.

Finally, compared with the other approaches briefly surveyed in this
section, Darné et al. (2015) propose a rigorous and flexible methodological framework to select and calibrate initial shocks to be used in bank
stress test scenarios based on statistical techniques for detecting outliers
in time-series of risk factors. Their approach allows characterizing not
only the magnitude but also the persistence of the initial shock. In this
chapter, based on our earlier work in Darné et al. (2015), we focus on
the calibration of *initial* shocks at the very early stage of the stress testing
exercise. The main empirical questions we want to address are: "What
should be the appropriate length of the stress period?"; "What are
the most appropriate reverting dynamics for the initial shocks to risk
factors if they are supposed transitory?"; "Are these reverting patterns
specific to the considered risk factors or to the stress horizon?"

6.3 A New Approach to Select Shock Scenarios

In this section we sketch the intuition behind a novel statistical approach
proposed by Darné et al. (2015). The technical details of the approach,
as well as several numerical illustrations, are discussed at length in the
aforementioned reference. The basic idea is that the initial shocks considered at the very early stage of a stress testing exercise may be viewed
as the materialization of rare or exceptional events that affect dramatically the dynamics of relevant risk factors. Defined in this way, they
may be represented as *outliers* in time-series econometrics. Outliers are
practically present in almost all economic and financial time-series and
are due to exceptionally rare events that cause sudden shifts in the level
of variables. In time-series econometrics, the statistical techniques conceived to detect and characterize outliers are based on the so-called
"intervention analysis" applied to linear models (see the seminal works
by Box and Tiao 1975; Tsay 1988; and Balke and Fomby 1994).

According to Chen and Liu's (1993) classification that has become
standard in the literature, the outliers may be categorized into four
distinct classes:

- *Additive outliers* (AOs), which have a "one-shot" effect on the
  observed series. They affect a single observation at a given point in
  time, without influencing any other subsequent observation.

- *Innovative outliers* (IOs), which appear as atypical observations in the noise process and affect the time-series only temporarily.
- *Level shifts* (LSs), which increase or decrease all the observations from a certain point in time onward by some constant level, producing abrupt and persistent changes to the series.
- *Temporary or transitory changes* (TC), which produce an initial shock to the series and then the effect vanishes with passing time.

By isomorphism, "level shifts" correspond to "permanent shocks," while "temporary changes" correspond to "transitory shocks" in the stress testing terminology. Intuitively, the outlier detection algorithms consist of fitting recursively a sequence of autoregressive integrated moving average (ARIMA) models to the observed series of a selected risk factor and using the residuals to detect the various types of outliers. The detection procedure, which is purely statistical in scope, is based on likelihood ratio tests performed separately, for each observation and for each type of outlier. Once an outlier is detected, the effect on the series is removed from the data and the detection procedure is rerun recursively until no more outliers are found (see Darné et al., 2015, for more technical details).

6.4 A Simple Illustration

In Darné, Levy-Rueff, and Pop (2015), we discuss several numerical illustrations of the outlier detection algorithms using various series of risk factors communally considered in the practice of stress testing: macroeconomic series (e.g., shocks to the GDP); real estate prices; inflation rates; interest rates and yields; and commodity prices. This section sketches the basic intuitions behind the outlier detection procedure and discusses a simple illustration of implementing the proposed methodology by calibrating shocks to real estate prices.

In the practice of stress tests, there are two types of shocks that are regularly considered (see, e.g., Martin and Tiesset 2009):

- *Transitory shocks*, which are implemented gradually over the considered stressed period. The idea here is that after some time (e.g., several quarters, depending on the presumed persistence of the initial shock) the stressed variable follows a reverting process toward the long-term trend that is reached at the end of the stress testing horizon.

- *Permanent shocks*, which are maintained at the same stressed level throughout the entire considered stress period. Market or monetary policy scenarios (e.g., exchange rate shocks; yield curve shocks) are the most common examples of this kind of shocks.

The advantage of the outlier detection–based approach is that the nature of the shock may be inferred *endogenously* instead of supposing it as given on an ad hoc basis. Specifically, this is done by characterizing the dynamics of the identified outlier in the time-series of risk drivers. In the particular case of a *transitory* shock, the proposed methodology allows us to jointly characterize the *severity* of the shock and the stress *horizon*. As such, the *severity of the shock* may be characterized in an intuitive way as the maximum spread between the *observed* and the *corrected*, outlier-free, risk factor series around the detection date. In the same manner, the *stress horizon* may be defined as the time frame between the first materialization of the shock – i.e., the first point in time when the *observed* and *outlier-free* series start to diverge – and the date of the reversal to the long-term trend.

For illustration purposes, we select one series that exhibits interesting and interpretable reverting patterns ("transitory changes"). A common stressed variable used in stress tests is the real estate (commercial and residential property) prices. Figure 6.1 presents the evolution of a broad US property index (quarterly time series). By applying the outlier detection procedure, we are able to detect a short extreme movement in the property index at the beginning of the 1990s and a more severe shock to the series during the first quarter of 2008 due to the worsening mortgage crisis in the United States.

The reverting pattern (transitory change, TC) depicted in Figure 6.1 implies a length of the stress horizon of two years (or eight quarters) and a magnitude of the shock of about –10%. These figures are in line with the proposed values used to calibrate macro stress testing exercises (see also BGFRS, 2014).

By applying the outlier detection algorithms to other series usually considered in the practice of stress testing, we show in Darné et al. (2015) that the dynamics of shocks, the length of the stress horizon, and the shock severity, are quite sensitive to the type of initial shock and the nature of the risk factor. For instance, it seems that the inferred stress horizon is relatively longer (one to two years) for macroeconomic risk factors (e.g., GDP, inflation rates, real estate and oil prices),

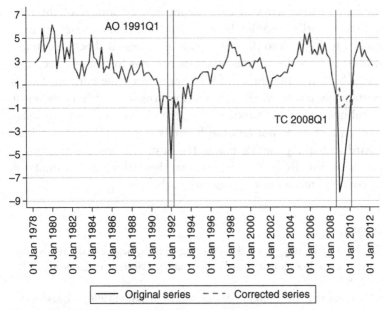

Figure 6.1 Outliers detection in property prices.

Note: this figure shows the original and corrected, outlier-free, series of a broad US property index from Bloomberg, as well as the identified outliers (additive outlier, AO, and transitory change, TC).

compared with interest rate variables and the slope of the yield curve (six months).

To conclude this section, we would like to mention a general issue related to the interpretation of the shocks and the implementation of the outlier detection algorithms that deserves further investigation. Particularly, what kind of initial shocks are more dangerous, long lasting and severe, but *isolated*, shocks or short-lived and moderate shocks, which are *clustered* over a relatively short period?

6.5 Conclusion

In this chapter, we propose a discussion of the growing economic literature on stress testing, with a particular focus on the methodologies used to calibrate shocks and scenarios. We also present a rigorous and flexible methodological framework to select initial shocks to be used in stress scenarios based on statistical techniques for detection of outliers in time-series of risk factors. The advantage of the proposed framework is twofold. First, it allows us to characterize not only the magnitude, but also the persistence of the initial shock. Second, it allows us to consider various reverting patterns for the stressed variables and informs the choice of the appropriate time horizon. This is important because extreme but plausible stresses that have the most harmful impact on the banking sector are of the transitory but long-lasting type; they do not necessarily imply structural changes, which are hard to make plausible before the bust, but keep having effects during a sufficiently long period, so that they cannot be dissimulated by accounting techniques or regulatory arbitrage.

References

Balke, N. and Fomby, T. (1994). Shifting Trends, Segmented Trends, and Infrequent Permanent Shocks. *Journal of Monetary Economics*, 28, 61–85.

Basel Committee on Banking Supervision (BCBS). (1996). Amendment to the Capital Accord to Incorporate Market Risks. Basel: Bank for International Settlements.

Basel Committee on Banking Supervision (BCBS). (2006). International Convergence of Capital Measurement and Capital Standards: A Revised Framework. Basel: Bank for International Settlements.

Basel Committee on Banking Supervision (BCBS). (2009). Principles for Sound Stress Testing Practices and Supervision. Basel: Bank for International Settlements.

Blaschke, W., Jones, M.T., Majnoni, G. and Peria, S.M. (2001). Stress Testing of Financial Systems: An Overview of Issues, Methodologies, and FSAP Experiences, IMF working paper, 01/88.

Board of Governors of the Federal Reserve System (BGFRS). (2014). 2015 Supervisory Scenarios for Annual Stress Tests Required under the Dodd–Frank Act Stress Testing Rules and the Capital Plan Rule. Released on October 23rd.

Borio, C. and Drehmann, M. (2009). Towards an Operational Framework for Financial Stability: 'Fuzzy' Measurement and its Consequences. BIS Working Paper 284. Basel: Bank for International Settlements.

Borio, C., Drehmann, M., and Tsatsaronis, K. (2014). Stress-testing Macro Stress Testing: Does It Live Up to Expectations? *Journal of Financial Stability*, 12, 3–15.

Boss, M., Breuer, T., Elsinger, H., Jandacka, M., Krenn, G., Lehar, A., Puhr, C., and Summer, M. (2006). Systemic Risk Monitor: A Model for Systemic

Risk Analysis and Stress Testing of Banking Systems. Technical Report. Vienna: Oesterreichische Nationalbank.

Box, G. and Tiao, G. (1975). Intervention Analysis with Applications to Economic and Environmental Problems. *Journal of the American Statistical Association*, 70, 70–79.

Breuer, T. and Csiszár, I. (2013). Systematic Stress Tests with Entropic Plausibility Constraints. *Journal of Banking and Finance*, 37, 1552–1559.

Breuer, T., Jandačka, M., Mencía, J., and Summer, M. (2012). A Systematic Approach to Multi-period Stress Testing of Portfolio Credit Risk. *Journal of Banking and Finance*, 36:2, 332–340.

Breuer, T., Jandačka, M., Rheinberger, K., and Summer M. (2009). How to Find Plausible, Severe, and Useful Stress Scenarios. *International Journal of Central Banking*, 5, 205–224.

Bunn, P., Cunningham, A., and Drehmann, M. (2005). Stress Testing as a Tool for Assessing Systemic Risks. Bank of England, Financial Stability Review.

Chen, C. and Liu, L. (1993). Joint Estimation of Model Parameters and Outlier Effects in Time Series. *Journal of the American Statistical Association*, 88, 284–297.

Cihak, M. (2004). Stress Testing: A Review of Key Concepts. Working Paper. Prague: Czech National Bank.

(2007). Introduction to Applied Stress Testing. IMF Working Paper No. 59. Washington, DC: International Monetary Fund.

Committee of European Banking Supervisors (CEBS). (2010). Aggregate Outcome of the 2010 EU Wide Stress Test Exercise. London: CEBS.

Committee on the Global Financial System (CGFS). (2000). Stress Testing by Large Financial Institutions: Current Practice and Aggregation Issues. CGFS Publications No. 14. Basel: Bank for International Settlements.

Committee on the Global Financial System (CGFS). (2001). A Survey of Stress Tests and Current Practice at Major Financial Institutions. CGFS Publications No. 18. Basel: Bank for International Settlements.

Committee on the Global Financial System (CGFS). (2005). Stress Testing at Major Financial Institutions: Survey Results and Practices. CGFS Publications No. 24. Basel: Bank for International Settlements.

Darné, O., Levy-Rueff, G., and Pop, A. (2015). Calibrating Initial Shocks in Bank Stress Test Scenarios: An Outlier Detection Based Approach. Paper presented at the University of Kent and Bank of Finland Conference "From the Last Financial Crisis to the Next."

De Bandt, O. and Oung, V. (2004). Assessment of Stress Tests Conducted on the French Banking System. *Banque de France, Financial Stability Review*, 5, 55–72.

Drehmann, M. (2008). Stress Tests: Objectives, Challenges, and Modelling Choices. *Riksbank Economic Review*, 2, 60–92.

(2009).Macroeconomic Stress-testing Banks: A Survey of Methodologies.In M. Quagliariello (ed.), *Stress-testing the Banking System: Methodologies and Applications*, pp. 37–67. Cambridge: Cambridge University Press.

Drehmann, M., Borio, C., and Tsatsaronis, K. (2012). Characterising the Financial Cycle: Don't Lose Sight of the Medium Term. BIS Working Paper No. 380. Basel: Bank for International Settlements.

Drehmann, M., Sorensen, S., and Stringa, M. (2008). The Integrated Impact of Credit and Interest Rate Risk on Banks: An Economic Value and Capital Adequacy Perspective, Working Paper No. 339, Bank of England.

Dubecq, S. and Gourieroux, C. (2012). Shock on Variable or Shock on Distribution with Application to Stress-Tests. Banque de France Working Paper No. 368.

European Banking Authority (EBA). (2011). EU-wide Stress Test Aggregate Report 2011.

European Banking Authority (EBA). (2014). EU-wide Stress Test Aggregate Report 2014.

European Insurance and Occupational Pension Authority (EIOPA). (2011). Specifications for the 2011 EU-wide Stress Test in the Insurance Sector. March.

Financial Services Authority (FSA). (2006). Stress Testing Thematic Review. Letter to Chief Executives, October.

Foglia, A. (2009). Stress Testing Credit Risk: A Survey of Authorities' Approaches. *International Journal of Central Banking*, 5:3, 9–45.

Haldane, A. (2009). Why Banks Failed the Stress Test? Speech, Bank of England.

Isogai, T. (2009). Scenario Design and Calibration. In M. Quagliariello (ed.), *Stress-testing the Banking System: Methodologies and Applications*, pp. 68–79. Cambridge: Cambridge University Press.

Jokivuolle, E., Virén, M., and Vähämaa, O. (2010). Transmission of Macro Shocks to Loan Losses in a Deep Crisis: The Case of Finland. In D. Rösch and H. Scheule (eds.), *Model Risk: Identification, Measurement and Management*, pp. 183–208. London: Risk Books.

Martin, C. and Tiesset, M. (2009). From the Macro to the Micro: The French Experience on Credit Risk Stress Testing. In M. Quagliariello (ed.), *Stress-testing the Banking System: Methodologies and Applications*, pp. 238–260. Cambridge: Cambridge University Press.

Schuermann, T. (2014). Stress Testing Banks. *International Journal of Forecasting*, 30, 717–728.

Sorge, M. (2004). Stress-testing Financial Systems: An Overview of Current Methodologies. Working Paper No. 165. Basel: Bank for International Settlements.

Sorge, M. and Virolainen, K. (2006). A Comparative Analysis of Macro Stress-testing Methodologies with Application to Finland. *Journal of Financial Stability*, 2, 113–151.

Tsay, R. (1988). Outliers, Level Shifts, and Variance Changes in Time Series. *Journal of Forecasting*, 7, 1–20.

Varotto, S. (2012). Stress Testing Credit Risk: The Great Depression Scenario. *Journal of Banking and Finance*, 36:12, 3133–3149.

7 | Making Sense of the EU-Wide Stress Test – Comparing SRISK and the ECB/EBA Measures of Bank Vulnerability

TIMOTEJ HOMAR, HEINRICH KICK
AND CARMELO SALLEO

7.1 Introduction

When the results of the European Central Bank (ECB) Comprehensive Assessment (CA) were published, the exercise was proclaimed a success by policymakers. At the same time, in a series of policy papers Acharya and Steffen (2014a,b,c) use SRISK as a benchmark of appropriate stress to cast doubt on its robustness. They point at the negative correlation between ECB/European Banking Authority (EBA) stress test shortfalls and SRISK, questioning whether the CA has properly taken into account systemic risk (Steffen 2014) and suggesting that the use of risk-weighted assets and discretion of national regulators could have affected the results of the ECB/EBA stress test (Acharya and Steffen 2014c). In an earlier study Acharya, Engle and Pierret (2014) used SRISK to compare it with stress test results conducted in the United States (SCAP) and the European Union (EBA stress test of 2011). They present SRISK as a robust, easy to use benchmark for macroprudential stress tests, quoting the high correlation of SRISK and stress test shortfalls in the majority of past US and EBA stress tests.

We take the discrepancies between the SRISK measure and the ECB stress test results as an occasion to perform an anatomy lesson of these measures of capital shortfall in a stress scenario.

Disclaimer: The views expressed in this chapter are not necessarily the same as those of the ECB and merely represent those of the authors.

Acknowledgements: The authors would like to thank Paul Bochmann and Joachim Eule, who provided outstanding and invaluable research assistance. The current version has benefitted from comments provided by Marco Pagano on a related internal note, from Christian Schlag and Radu Tunaru.

The two measures take a fundamentally different approach to engineer the stress test impact on bank capital. While the ECB stress test starts by specifying a macro scenario and possible shocks to the financial markets and derives key metrics for credit losses such as probability of default and loss given default for loans, SRISK infers the stress impact from long-term covariance of bank stock returns with market returns, specifying the initial shock in terms of a decline in the stock market. It thereby sidesteps modelling the transmission mechanisms of macroeconomic developments to bank risk metrics and then to bank losses explicitly and rather models directly banks losses. Proponents of the market-based perspective would argue that although not modelling the transmission channels and a sophisticated stress scenario, assuming that a severe downturn at the stock market is a reflection of a severe crisis, the information contained in the thus modelled bank losses implicitly accounts for all the relevant transmission channels. This arguably might bear fewer sources of mistakes or omissions of risks factors, as the market processes the entire information set. In particular, complex contagion mechanisms that are notoriously difficult to model, such as illiquidity spirals, fire sale externalities and information contagion, are all implicitly reflected in market prices, to the extent that the market is aware of these channels. Its conceptual problems lie within the assumptions that the model for the long-term co-variation between bank returns and market returns remains valid for a long horizon and during significant stress on the banking system, which need not be the case when the market's information set changes.

While the success of a stress test, as discussed in Borio, Drehmann and Tsatsaronis (2014), depends on the function it was designed for, the quality of a macro stress test hinges on the plausibility and severity of the scenario and its translation into stress test impact (Alfaro and Drehmann 2009). Ideally, the stress test impact should reflect banks' exposures to a number of risks, most importantly credit risk due to macro and micro factors and trading risks related to market exposures. This motivates an investigation of the stress impacts of both the ECB CA and SRISK to examine how they relate to a set of factors that explain bank fragility. While the previous comparisons of SRISK and ECB/EBA stress test results cited here compare the shortfalls directly, we focus on the impact of the stress scenarios employed by the ECB and by Acharya and Steffen (2014a,b) instead of the capital shortfalls. We normalise the dollar amount of stress impact by a common notion of firm exposure. The normalised measures capture the losses associated with the stress scenario as a fraction of exposure, which effectively defines the stress test; the shortfalls follow mechanically after defining the hurdle rate and the particular measure of leverage.

We proceed by regressing the stress impacts of both measures on a set of macro variables, bank balance sheet variables and market-based measures to understand the drivers behind the stress scenarios. We regard this exercise as an anatomy lesson of the stress test measures, which should facilitate an assessment of their plausibility and their relationship to economic reality.

In Section 7.2 we provide some background about the ECB/EBA stress test and SRISK. Section 7.3 describes the data. Results about the ECB/EBA stress test are in Section 7.4. Section 7.5 compares SRISK to ECB/EBA stress test outcomes and Section 7.6 concludes.

7.2 The ECB/EBA Stress Test and the SRISK Measure

The ECB/EBA stress test was conducted on 130 Eurozone banks as a part of the CA in 2014. A distinguishing feature of this stress test, compared to the previous ones, is that it incorporates corrections to asset valuation and classifications that resulted from the asset quality review (AQR), which was also part of the CA. The stress test itself combined a bottom-up stress test with a top-down verification, thereby achieving harmonisation across participating banks and verifying the results that were subject to each bank's discretion. The baseline scenario was constructed based on European Commission forecasts for the years 2014–2016. The European Systemic Risk Board modified the baseline scenario by the materialisation of the main risks to financial stability to arrive at the adverse scenario.[1] EBA then published the stress test methodology, where key stress parameters were derived from the scenarios and restrictions were imposed on the banks' application of the scenario. The results thus obtained were cross-checked with the outcome of a macro stress test to detect misuse of banks' discretion. The main outcome of the stress test is the capital shortfall, defined as the maximum of the capital needed to meet a common equity Tier 1 (CET1) ratio of 8% in the baseline scenario or a CET1 ratio of

---

[1] For details see EBA/SSM stress test: The macroeconomic adverse scenario (ESRB 2014).

5.5% in the adverse scenario, where CET1 is measured according to the respective legislation in each year. The results are published in the Aggregate Report on the Comprehensive Assessment (ECB 2014). Rather than on the shortfall, we focus on the stress impact, i.e. the loss of bank capital in the stress scenario. The shortfall shows which banks are most undercapitalised, while the stress impact is more informative about bank exposure to risks.

SRISK has been proposed as a measure of systemic risk by Acharya, Engle and Richardson (2012). SRISK of a bank is the expected capital shortfall in a severe stress scenario with respect to a benchmark capital ratio defined in terms of market leverage. For European banks the threshold is 5.5% market leverage ratio.[2] The stress scenario is a shock that would result in a 40% drop in the general stock market index over a period of six months. More precisely, SRISK is defined as

$$\text{SRISK}_{it} = E_t(CS_{i,t+h} \mid R_{mt+1:t+h} < C) \tag{7.1}$$

where CS denotes capital shortfall and R_m refers to the return of the market index. The systemic event is thus defined as a drop in the market over the term of six months below the threshold C, where C is taken to be -40 %. This is shown by the authors to result in the following expression:

$$\text{SRISK}_{it} = k\,\text{Debt}_{it} - (1-k)\,\text{Equity}_{it}\left(1 + \text{LRMES}_{it}\right) \tag{7.2}$$

where k denotes the capital requirement and Debt is the book value of all liabilities except capital. LRMES stands for long-run marginal expected shortfall and is extrapolated from the mean daily marginal expected shortfall (MES)[3] to a six-month horizon via simulations. LRMES*Equity can be interpreted as the stress impact in euros. Normalising it by total assets yields the SRISK stress impact:

$$\frac{\text{SRISK}_{\text{Stress Impact}}}{TA_{\text{Book}}} = \text{LRMES} * \frac{\text{Equity}_{\text{Market}}}{TA_{\text{Market}}} * \frac{TA_{\text{Market}}}{TA_{\text{Book}}} \tag{7.3}$$

[2] Market leverage ratio is defined as market value of equity divided by market value of assets, which is approximated as the sum of market value of equity and book value of liabilities.
[3] MES in turn is defined as $\text{MES}_{i,t} = E_t\left(r_{i,t+1} \mid r_{m,t+1} < C\right)$, which is in perfect analogy to the LRMES except for a time horizon of one day. Brownlees and Engle propose a Dynamic Conditional Correlation–Generalized AutoRegressive Conditional Heteroskedasticity (DCC-GARCH) model to estimate the MES.

There are two ways of obtaining this stress impact from the data provided on the webpage of V-Lab. Acharya et al. (2012) mention an approximation to LRMES: $LRMES = 1 - \exp(-18 \times MES)$, which they employ in cases where simulations have not yet been implemented. Alternatively, using the SRISK measure as a starting point, we can back out the impact of the stress test on market equity as follows:

$$\frac{SRISK_{\text{Stress Impact}}}{TA_{\text{Book}}} = \left(\frac{\text{Equity}_{\text{Market}}}{TA_{\text{Market}}} - 0.055 \right) \left(\frac{TA_{\text{Market}}}{TA_{\text{Book}}} \right)$$
$$+ \frac{SRISK_{\text{Shortfall}}}{TA_{\text{Book}}} \tag{7.4}$$

where $\text{Equity}_{\text{Market}}$ stands for market value of equity and TA_{Market} for market value of total assets (the sum of market value of equity and book value of liabilities). $SRISK_{\text{Shortfall}}$ is the capital shortfall in EUR, which has a positive value when a bank has too little equity and negative when it has a surplus. The first expression is the difference between the initial market leverage ratio and the benchmark leverage ratio, rescaled from market value of total assets to book value of total assets. Then the shortfall after the shock is added. If a bank has an initial market leverage ratio above 5.5% and has a shortfall after the shock, the stress impact is the loss of capital from the initial level with respect to the benchmark capital ratio plus the shortfall. If a bank is below the benchmark market leverage ratio before the shock, the stress impact is equal to the shortfall after the shock reduced for the initial shortfall. Cross-checking results obtained from these methods, see Table 7.1, confirms that any disagreement due the approximation involved or different data used is insignificant, so we go ahead with the values obtained via the second method, described by Eq. (7.4).

7.3 Data and Descriptive Statistics

7.3.1 Endogenous Variables

We obtained data about the ECB/EBA stress test results from the Aggregate Report on the Comprehensive Assessment (ECB 2014) and data on banking and trading book losses from EBA. We used the following stress test outcomes as dependent variables in the regression analysis:

Table 7.1 *Comparison of ECB/EBA stress impact an SRISK stress impact*

	ECB/EBA stress test impact	SRISK stress impact
Calculation	[ECB/EBA stress on CET1] * RWA/TA	$\left(\dfrac{\text{Equity}_{\text{Market}}}{TA_{\text{Market}}} - 0.055\right)\left(\dfrac{TA_{\text{Market}}}{TA_{\text{Book}}}\right) + \dfrac{\text{SRISK}_{\text{Shortfall}}}{TA_{\text{Book}}}$
Economic interpretation of stress	Losses associated with adverse macroeconomic conditions (GDP, inflation) and adverse conditions on the financial markets (yields, equity, FX) – mainly losses related to credit risk.	Losses associated with any event that causes the aggregated stock market to drop by 40% – covers any financial market shock that is severe enough.
Transmis-sion mechanism	Weak macro conditions such as high unemployment, recession, low inflation increase the probability that borrowers default on their loans, and the losses in that case (reduced collateral values), with the adverse conditions to the financial markets, lead to market gains or losses on the banks' trading portfolios.	Not explicitly modelled
Static balance sheet assumption	Yes	Yes (in the sense that debt is not reduced – the composition of assets and liabilities could change significantly in terms of risk and liquidity profile).
Perspective	All stakeholders, losses to assets.	Equity holders, losses to market equity.
Direct and indirect contagion	Not modelled and therefore not part of the scenario.	Not modelled explicitly, but potentially the modelling of the impact of the stress on the bank's equity includes contagion and spillovers from other parts of the financial markets.

- *Adverse scenario stress impact/TA*: Impact of the adverse scenario of the ECB/EBA stress test on CET1 (ECB communication variable B6), scaled by total assets. Stress impact is originally reported in basis points of risk-weighted assets (RWA). We rescale it and express it in percent of total assets. Normalizing the stress impact by some measure of bank size is necessary to make it comparable across banks. If one could argue that the stress impact on an asset class should be proportional to its RWA, expressing it relative to RWA would be preferable. We perform regressions with stress impact scaled by RWA as a robustness check.
- *Baseline scenario stress impact/TA*: Impact of the baseline scenario of the ECB/EBA stress test on CET1 (ECB communication variable B4), scaled by total assets. We focus on the adverse scenario stress impact, which has greater variation in outcomes across banks, and analyse the impact of the baseline scenario in robustness checks.
- *Banking book losses/TA*: Three-year cumulative losses on financial and non-financial assets in the banking book in the adverse scenario, scaled by total assets. By isolating the losses on the credit portfolio from the trading activities, one would expect to see more clearly the influences of the macroeconomic stress scenario that ultimately translates into probability of default and loss given default metrics of loan portfolios.
- *Trading book losses/securities holdings*: Three-year cumulative losses in the trading book in the adverse scenario, scaled by total assets.

The adverse scenario stress impact/TA is the measure we refer to in most of what follows – the other measures have been analysed in the robustness checks (not shown). We comment on any noteworthy qualitative differences without giving the quantitative details.

We compute the *SRISK stress impact/TA* using Equation (7.4) from SRISK values published on the V-Lab website.[4] By transforming the dollar values of SRISK shortfall, as they were originally reported, into stress impact scaled by total assets we make it directly comparable to the ECB/EBA stress impact.

---

[4] http://vlab.stern.nyu.edu/en/# – the data provided include the dollar amounts of SRISK for a sample of forty-three significant institutions covering around 66% of total assets under direct SSM supervision. This is the only variable we need to use from that source.

7.3.2 Exogenous Variables

Losses in a stress scenario are likely to depend on the existing *macro-economic conditions*. For some variables we construct values weighted by exposure of banks to different countries to account for the fact that banks are likely to be affected by macroeconomic conditions not only in the country of their headquarters but also in countries where they have asset exposure – i.e. the effect of macroeconomic conditions in a particular country on a bank is assumed to be proportional to the exposure of the bank to that country relative to the total assets of the bank.[5] In the regression analysis we use the following variables:

- Real gross domestic product (GDP) growth, three-year cumulated for the period 2011–2013 and weighted by bank exposures (source: IMF World Economic Outlook)
- Sovereign bond yields, average of monthly observations for 2013 (source: Bloomberg)
- Unemployment rate, three-year average (source: Eurostat, obtained through ECB SDW)
- Expected default frequency (EDF) for nonfinancial firms, country benchmark, average over firms weighted by total assets, average of monthly observations for 2013, weighted by bank exposures (ECB SDW,[6] source: KMV – Moody's)

We use *quality of banking supervision* measures from Barth, Caprio and Levine (2012). Variables are constructed as averages over up to four survey waves ranging back until 1999. Higher index levels imply tighter regulation.

- The bank activities restrictions index describes how much activities of banks are restricted to providing core banking services. The index is higher when banks are, for example, prohibited from engaging in securities underwriting, brokering or dealing, insurance underwriting, real estate investment or if banks are not allowed to own non-financial firms.
- The capital regulatory index is higher the more stringent regulatory requirements for holding capital are. It also measures how narrowly capital is defined.

---

[5] For details about weighting macroeconomic variables by bank exposures see Appendix 7.1.
[6] ECB Statistical Data Warehouse.

- The supervisory power index measures whether supervisory authorities have the power to prevent and correct problems. For example, the index is higher if authorities can restructure and reorganise troubled banks or declare a deeply troubled bank insolvent.
- The private monitoring index is high when financial statements issued by a bank have to be audited, when a large share of the ten largest banks is rated by international rating agencies, when there is no explicit deposit insurance scheme and if bank accounting fulfils certain requirements.
- The moral hazard mitigation index measures the extent to which features of the explicit deposit insurance reduce moral hazard, i.e. that the funding modalities of a bank do not discourage a bank from engaging in high-risk lending. A high value implies that the deposit insurance system has been designed to be effective in mitigating moral hazard, for instance by charging banks for the insurance scheme proportional to their risk, or by insuring less than 100% of the deposits.

Bank balance sheet variables are combined from three sources. If available, we use variables from the dataset accompanying the report about the CA (ECB 2014). Additional variables are from SNL and BankScope. For some banks SNL and BankScope are used simultaneously when total assets in both datasets do not differ by more than 10%.

- Bank size, measured as the logarithm of total assets (source: CA report)
- Tier 1 ratio (source: CA report)
- Book leverage ratio: book value of equity divided by total assets (source: CA report)
- RWA to total assets ratio (source: CA report)
- Gross loans excluding interbank loans (source: SNL, BankScope)
- Securities holdings (source: SNL, BankScope)
- ROA (return on average assets) (source: SNL, BankScope)
- Impaired loans ratio: impaired loans over gross loans (source: SNL, BankScope)

Market data are compiled from Bloomberg unless specified otherwise:

- Bank five-year credit default swap (CDS) spreads, average over end-of-month observations in 2013

- Price to book ratio, end of 2013
- Market leverage ratio: market value of equity over the sum of market value of equity and book value of liabilities (source: V-Lab)
- Bank stock returns for the period 2011–2013.[7]
- Bank stock four-factor alpha: average daily abnormal return over the period 2011–2013, computed as the intercept from the Carhart (1997) four-factor asset pricing model, which builds on the Fama-French (1993) three-factor model and augments it with another factor capturing the momentum effect. We use the return on Eurostoxx50 as a proxy for market return and the German five-year government bond yield as the risk-free rate. The other three factors are taken from Andrea Frazzini's data library.[8]

The sample of banks subject to the AQR and the stress test consists of 130 banks, but we remove four banks[9] where we have no observations on the explanatory variables in the most basic setup. The descriptive statistics of the full sample are displayed in Table 7.2. Most explanatory variables are available for at least 120 banks, which represent 96% or more of total assets of banks that were analysed in the CA. For variables based on market data the coverage is more limited and includes about forty banks, which account for 50% to 67% of total banking assets. SRISK is available for a sample covering 62% of the assets of banks examined in the ECB/EBA stress test.

7.4 Analysis of the ECB/EBA Adverse Scenario Stress Impact

The results presented in this section identify several factors that predict bank vulnerability, as measured by the ECB/EBA adverse scenario stress impact on Tier 1 capital. Table 7.2 displays the results for the total adverse scenario stress impact. Columns (1) to (4) in Table 7.3 report results for regressions with variables describing macroeconomic

---

[7] For variables based on stock returns, only stocks that have zero returns on fewer than 50%s of the trading days are considered. Stocks that have zero returns on more days may have been suspended from trading or are highly illiquid and thus not suitable for analysis.

[8] Available at www.aqr.com/library/data-sets/the-devil-in-hmls-details-factors-daily (Asness and Frazzini 2013).

[9] Deutsche Bank (Malta), AB SEB Bankas Latvia, AB DNB Bankas Latvia and Swedbank AB, Latvia, jointly representing 0.01% of sample assets.

Table 7.2 *Adverse scenario stress impact*

	Adv. scen. stress impact/TA	Adv. scen. stress impact/TA	Adv. scen. stress impact/TA	Adv. scen. stress impact/TA	Adv. scen. stress impact/TA	Adv. scen. stress impact/TA
	(1)	(2)	(3)	(4)	(5)	(6)
GDP growth, 3-year	-11.8112*** (-3.47)			-7.7331*** (-3.02)		-19.5453*** (-5.32)
Govt. bond yield		33.0032*** (5.37)				
EDF nonfin. Sector			10.7192 (0.73)			
Unemployment, 3-year average			4.5003 (0.78)			
Bank activity restr. ind.	-0.3765** (-2.31)	-0.4091** (-2.43)	-0.3019 (-1.12)	-0.4416*** (-4.03)	-0.2726* (-2.02)	-0.3996* (-2.17)
Capital regulatory ind.	-0.3659* (-2.07)	-0.3987** (-2.55)	-0.4216 (-1.31)	-0.5170*** (-3.75)	-0.2400* (-2.08)	-0.3202* (-1.89)
Size	-0.2685*** (-3.21)	-0.2371* (-1.88)	-0.2566** (-2.54)	-0.2432*** (-3.25)	-0.2744** (-2.42)	-0.2469* (-2.00)
Book leverage ratio	-4.1229 (-0.99)	-7.0662 (-1.59)	-9.6953* (-1.88)	-5.0698 (-1.32)	-9.8820 (-0.83)	-9.1439 (-0.67)

	(1)	(2)	(3)	(4)	(5)	(6)
Loans/TA	-1.1830*	-0.9124	-1.1920	-1.2594*	-1.5578*	-1.7908
	(-2.01)	(-1.28)	(-1.50)	(-1.77)	(-2.07)	(-1.05)
RWA/TA	2.8346***	2.2486***	2.9307***	1.8523**	2.5746*	-0.0314
	(4.10)	(3.38)	(3.57)	(2.57)	(2.12)	(-0.02)
ROA	-27.2224**	-33.1259***	-39.0208***	-14.6771	-17.6079	-10.3840
	(-2.77)	(-3.90)	(-4.60)	(-1.37)	(-1.40)	(-0.91)
Impaired loans ratio				5.5447***		
				(4.51)		
Bank CDS spread					0.3450***	
					(7.12)	
Bank stock four-factor alpha						-3.7657*
						(-1.89)
N of observations	121	108	105	105	51	41
Coverage of bank assets (%)	98.33	97.36	88.01	92.08	67.71	48.63
Adjusted R^2	0.5082	0.5653	0.4350	0.6005	0.5965	0.5796

The dependent variable is adverse scenario stress impact scaled by total assets. Regressions are estimated using ordinary least squares (OLS) with standard errors clustered at country level. In parentheses are t-statistics. Significance levels of 0.10, 0.05 and 0.01 are denoted by *, **, ***, respectively.

Table 7.3 *Comparing the ECB adverse scenario stress impact and the SRISK stress impact: the importance of market leverage ratio*

	Adv. scen. stress impact/TA	Adv. scen. stress impact/TA	Adv. scen. stress impact/TA	SRISK stress impact/TA	SRISK stress impact/TA	SRISK stress impact/TA
	(1)	(2)	(3)	(4)	(5)	(6)
GDP growth, 3-year	−10.6212** (−2.32)	−4.8839 (−1.54)		21.3960 (0.97)	−5.7205 (−0.94)	
Bank activity restr. ind.	−0.5327*** (−3.07)	−0.3927* (−1.92)		−0.1994 (−0.28)	−0.3714 (−1.21)	
Capital regulatory ind.	−0.5001*** (−4.23)	−0.5059*** (−4.75)		−0.5840 (−1.37)	−0.2337 (−1.25)	
Size	−0.2443* (−1.95)	−0.2224 (−1.60)		0.4130 (0.91)	0.2982* (1.91)	
Loans/TA	−0.6676 (−0.51)	−0.2486 (−0.19)		3.7127 (0.80)	−0.1704 (−0.10)	
RWA/TA	3.3016** (2.41)	0.4674 (0.25)		−7.1147 (−0.95)	−0.4134 (−0.24)	
Impaired loans ratio	9.5597*** (7.46)	9.8883*** (6.54)		10.8675 (0.93)	−0.6279 (−0.44)	

	(1)	(2)	(3)	(4)	(5)
ROA	2.6278	1.9402		13.5989	−17.9481
	(0.33)	(0.22)		(1.02)	(−1.68)
Book leverage ratio	−36.1809*			85.1226	
	(−1.88)			(1.69)	
Market lev. ratio		−0.0547**	0.0158	0.5555***	0.5440***
		(−2.40)	(0.37)	(11.85)	(9.45)
N of observations	42	42	43	42	43
Coverage of bank assets (%)	61.96	61.96	62.07	61.96	62.07
Adjusted R^2	0.6575	0.6217	−0.0215	0.9126	0.8896

The dependent variables are the adverse scenario stress impact of the ECB stress test and the SRISK stress impact. Both are scaled by total assets. Regressions are estimated using OLS with standard errors clustered at country level. In parentheses are t-statistics. Significance levels of 0.10, 0.05 and 0.01 are denoted by *, **, ***, respectively.

conditions, quality of bank supervision and bank balance sheet varia-bles. Market-based measures, which are available only for a subsample of banks, are included in specifications (5) and (6). GDP growth and government bond yields have a significant effect on the stress impact in the adverse scenario. They are not included simultaneously because of their high correlation. Creditworthiness of nonfinancial corpora-tions, measured by the average expected default frequency (EDF) and unemployment rate do not have a significant effect. Restrictions on bank activities and more stringent capital requirements are associ-ated with lower stress impact. Looking at characteristics of individual banks, smaller banks are expected to be hit more.

Banks with riskier assets reflected in higher RWA ratio and high existing impaired loans are expected to suffer larger losses in the adverse scenario. Market-based measures, CDS spreads and abnormal returns on bank stock are very good predictors of stress impact.

Note that none of the explanatory variables except the market vari-ables carry any forward-looking component. This does by no means imply that they have no explanatory power for the stress test results, because they carry substantial information on the starting point of the scenario, and since most of the macrovariables have strong inertia the starting point already captures a significant amount of the cross-sectional heterogeneity of the macrovariables in a stress scenario, even without having a model for the future dynamics of the economy or the transmission mechanism. Furthermore, one would expect a significant part of a macro stress to be a common shock that affects all countries. The regressors do not contain any information about country-specific amplifiers of that common shock and how country specificities includ-ing different starting levels then introduce cross-country and cross-bank heterogeneity. The following results can therefore be understood as an analysis of how much of the information of the stress scenario is contained in information on the starting point of the scenario, and which of these initial conditions matter the most for the model-based outcome of a three-year stress scenario.

Overall, our results are in line with research linking credit losses to macroeconomic dynamics, such as, for instance Pesaran et al. (2006), Kearns (2004) and Mileris (2012). It is intuitive that the regressions explaining the banking book losses exhibit higher explanatory power than the regressions explaining the trading losses, as net trading posi-tions are far more heterogeneous across banks in a country than loan portfolio compositions, and also bear less systematic relation to balance sheet information apart from the size of the trading book, which is strictly negatively related to the loans over total assets ratio.

7.5 Comparing ECB/EBA Stress Test Outcomes with SRISK

Acharya and Steffen (2014c) find SRISK[10] to be negatively correlated with the shortfall of banks in the adverse scenario of the ECB/EBA stress test but positively correlated with the banking book and trading book losses in the adverse scenario of the same stress test. The stress scenarios of the two measures are different and the benchmark capital requirements differ (5.5 % market leverage ratio in SRISK and 5.5% CET1 ratio in the ECB/EBA stress test). Hence it is not surprising that the two shortfalls are not highly correlated.

Figure 7.1 illustrates the connection between the SRISK measure and the banking book losses and trading book losses, comparing both notional measures and our normalised stress impact measures. While the notional measures suggest a positive correlation, this is driven purely by the bank size, as the comparison of normalised measures clearly demonstrates. What are the origins of this disconnect between two measures that set out to measure in principle the same thing? The regression analysis in the following section will shed more light on the drivers of this counterintuitive finding.

SRISK is available only for publicly traded banks, limiting the regression sample to about forty banks corresponding to 50% of total banking assets covered by the CA. For comparison, both measures are regressed on three sets of regressors, allowing to accentuate the differences. Table 7.3 displays the results of the regressions of ECB stress impact (regressions (1), (2) and (3)) and of the SRISK stress impact (regressions (4), (5) and (6)) on the same set of variables and for an identical sample of banks.[11]

Two main observations can be made. First, the proportion of explained variance of the SRISK stress impact is very low when using those factors that best explained the adverse scenario impact, with

---

[10] The dollar value of SRISK shortfall is referred to just as SRISK.
[11] Note that the main relationships, the direction of signs, and often also significance levels, shown for the adverse scenario stress impacting on the full sample also hold for the reduced sample for which SRISK is available.

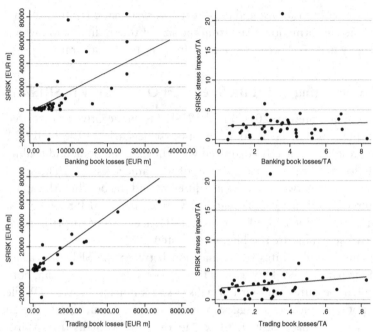

Figure 7.1 SRISK versus banking book losses and trading book losses, nominal values (left) and stress impact scaled by total assets (right).
The correlations calculated on the absolute values (left-hand side) are 0.6 (banking book losses) and 0.8 (trading book losses). They vanish to 0 and 0.1 respectively when normalised by total assets.

almost no statistically significant coefficients. Second, the book leverage ratio tremendously increases the explanatory power of the regression for the SRISK, but not for the ECB/EBA stress impact.

The reason for this is that the model underlying the SRISK measure does not properly account for losses that would wipe out the entire equity of a bank. Rather than modelling the loss of value of assets in case of a shock, as was done in the CA, SRISK models stock returns in case of a shock. In the ECB/EBA stress scenario, the losses under the stress scenario can exceed the capital a bank has prior to the stress. In contrast in the SRISK stress scenario, thinly capitalised banks may experience a large negative stock return, but their equity is not wiped out, however low it may be initially. This bounds the loss of value in the SRISK stress scenario to the initial market value of equity. As a result, the SRISK measure greatly underestimates the loss of value for banks with low initial capital and overestimates the losses for banks with high initial market value of equity. The loss of value expressed as a proportion of book total assets in the SRISK scenario is consequently best explained by the initial market leverage ratio of a bank: higher capitalised banks have more equity to lose, relative to total assets. Using the market leverage ratio instead of book leverage ratio does not materially affect estimates of regressions of the ECB stress impact. The estimated effect of market leverage ratio is negative, like the effect of book leverage ratio. Banks with more equity are expected to suffer lower losses. R^2 stays at the same level, at about 0.65.

The R^2 increases from 0.07 with book leverage ratio to 0.92 with market leverage ratio. In regression (6) market leverage ratio alone explains 89% of the variation in the SRISK stress impact, while it has virtually no explanatory power in case of the adverse scenario stress impact (column (3)). Banks with high initial market capitalisation lose much more value in the SRISK stress scenario than those with very low market capitalisation.

A positive link between market leverage ratio could be consistent with the explanation that banks with higher market equity have riskier portfolios. The relationship is, however, very strong and almost mechanical, suggesting it is due to the design of the SRISK measure. In order to understand this, it is imperative to recall the expression for SRISK stress impact provided earlier:

$$\frac{SRISK_{\text{Stress Impact}}}{TA_{\text{Book}}} = LRMES * \frac{Equity_{\text{Market}}}{TA_{\text{Market}}} * \frac{TA_{\text{Market}}}{TA_{\text{Book}}} \tag{7.5}$$

The first term results from long-term covariances with the market, and although better capitalised banks might engage in more risky behaviour than less well capitalised ones, there should be and is no strong relationship between leverage ratio and LRMES. The last term can be roughly approximated as 1, since there is typically no large discrepancy between book and market value of debt. While price to book ratio varies much more, it is effectively dominated by debt in the calculation of this ratio, as equity is a far smaller component of bank balance sheets than debt. The middle term is the market leverage ratio, which can be shown do display a large heterogeneity in our sample, effectively dominating the effect of the variation in LRMES.

Similarly, SRISK stress impact is also highly correlated with price to book ratio, which alone explains 47% of the variation in the SRISK

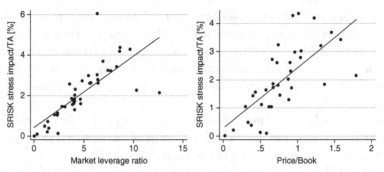

Figure 7.2 SRISK stress impact scaled by total assets vs. market leverage ratio (left) and price to book ratio (right).

The sample for the scatterplot with market leverage ratio does not include Allied Irish Banks, which is an outlier with a market leverage ratio of 36%. The observation of Allied Irish banks lies close to the fitted regression line so it does not affect the correlation. We do not plot it to prevent the other observations being collapsed to a small area of the plot.

stress scenario. Banks with larger price-to-book ratio are expected to suffer larger losses in the stress scenario. The correlations of SRISK stress impact with market leverage ratio and price to book ratio are depicted in Figure 7.2. Table 7.4 provides the regression results for price-to-book ratio. Book leverage ratio has a marginally significant negative effect on the stress impact of the ECB/EBA adverse scenario; the price-to-book ratio is insignificant. For SRISK stress impact, the price-to-book ratio has a highly significant positive effect.

In order to check, whether SRISK performs better when evaluated in a way it is originally modelled, i.e. in terms of stock returns, we scale SRISK stress impact by initial market capitalisation of banks and perform the same regression as before in robustness checks (not shown). Loss of value in the SRISK stress scenario divided by market capitalisation approximates the stock return over the six-month period in the SRISK stress scenario. GDP growth and quality of banking supervision measures now have significant effects with the expected negative sign.[12] However, the effects of market leverage ratio and price to book ratio are still dominant. In addition, the negative return on equity in the stress scenario seems to be smaller for banks with higher impaired loans ratio, which is in conflict with economic intuition.

[12] Note that a larger SRISK stress impact/initial market capitalisation should be interpreted as a negative stock return large in absolute value.

Table 7.4 Comparing the ECB adverse scenario stress impact and the SRISK stress impact: the importance of price to book ratio

	Adv. scen. stress impact/TA	Adv. scen. stress impact/TA	Adv. scen. stress impact/TA	SRISK stress impact/TA	SRISK stress impact/TA	SRISK stress impact/TA
	(1)	(2)	(3)	(4)	(5)	(6)
GDP growth, 3-year	−10.6212**	−16.0250***		21.3960	−8.5172***	
	(−2.52)	(−3.40)		(0.97)	(−4.13)	
Bank activity restr. ind.	−0.5327***	−0.3494		−0.1994	−0.3030**	
	(−3.07)	(−1.78)		(−0.28)	(−2.80)	
Capital regulatory ind.	−0.5001***	−0.2591		−0.5840	−0.1470*	
	(−4.23)	(−1.38)		(−1.37)	(−1.88)	
Size	−0.2443*	−0.2100		0.4130	0.3994***	
	(−1.95)	(−1.55)		(0.91)	(4.83)	
Loans/TA	−0.6676	−2.9656		3.7127	1.9461	
	(−0.51)	(−1.46)		(0.80)	(1.51)	
RWA/TA	3.3016**	3.8423**		−7.1147	1.4205	
	(2.41)	(2.88)		(−0.95)	(1.20)	
Impaired loans ratio	9.5597***	8.0456***		10.8675	−3.4866*	
	(7.46)	(3.97)		(0.93)	(−2.10)	

(continued)

127

Table 7.4 (cont.)

	Adv. scen. stress impact/TA	Adv. scen. stress impact/TA	Adv. scen. stress impact/TA	SRISK stress impact/TA	SRISK stress impact/TA	SRISK stress impact/TA
	(1)	(2)	(3)	(4)	(5)	(6)
ROA	2.6278	3.9402		13.5989	-0.4996	
	(0.33)	(0.37)		(1.02)	(-0.20)	
Book leverage ratio	-36.1809*	-39.4012*		85.1226	15.5929	
	(-1.88)	(-2.03)		(1.69)	(0.95)	
P/B ratio		-0.1464	-0.6767		2.2048***	2.1594***
		(-0.27)	(-0.76)		(11.15)	(4.37)
N of observations	42	35	36	42	35	36
Coverage of bank assets (%)	61.96	47.73	47.85	61.96	47.73	47.85
Adjusted R^2	0.6575	0.6376	-0.0006	0.0625	0.7288	0.4724

The dependent variables are the adverse scenario stress impact of the ECB stress test and the SRISK stress impact. Both are scaled by total assets. Regressions are estimated using OLS with standard errors clustered at country level. In parentheses are t-statistics. Significance levels of 0.10, 0.05 and 0.01 are denoted by *, **, ***, respectively.

To illustrate the extent to which the stress impact of the ECB stress test and the SRISK stress impact differ, Table 7.5 compares the adverse scenario stress impact and the SRISK stress impact, sorting banks by the ratio of the SRISK stress impact relative to the adverse scenario stress impact. This confirms that for the poorly capitalised banks such as Dexia, Hellenic Bank, Banca Monte Paschi di Sienna, etc., the SRISK stress impact is only a small fraction of the impact under the adverse stress scenario. Likewise, for the highly capitalised banks such as Nordea Bank Finland, the SRISK stress impact is higher than the impact of the ECB stress test by a factor of 10. When looking at the SRISK impact relative to the initial market capitalisation of a bank, i.e. the return equity investors would suffer in the stress scenario, the SRISK figures range from 10% 55%, which corresponds to the 40% drop in the general stock market. In contrast the range of losses in the SRISK stress scenario, relative to total assets spans from 0.96% to 21% of total assets of a bank. Given that small losses are associated with weakly capitalised banks and large ones with banks that have high market capitalisation relative to total assets, such dispersion clearly shows that the measure is unsuitable for estimating vulnerability of banks.

The stress impact in the adverse scenario of the ECB/EBA stress test shows the opposite pattern. Losses relative to total assets range from 0.06% to 7 %. Banks with low initial market value of equity lose a multiple of their equity value (up to 7400%) and well capitalised banks suffer only small losses relative to their market capitalisation (less than 10%).

7.6 Robustness Checks

To check the robustness of our results we perform additional regressions (not all results reported). First, we check whether scaling the stress impact by RWA instead of by total assets affects the results. Explanatory variables are the same as in Table 7.3 apart from that we use Tier 1 capital ratio instead of book capital ratio and do not include the risk-weighted to total assets ratio. Because the dependent variable is already scaled by RWA there is no need to include the RWA ratio as a control. The signs of estimated coefficients are mostly the same as when scaling by total assets. R^2 is noticeably lower. The effect of impaired loans is not significant and a higher Tier 1 ratio is associated

Table 7.5 *Comparison of the stress impact of the ECB/EBA adverse scenario with SRISK stress impact, by bank*

Bank	Total assets	Market leverage ratio	SRISK stress impact/TA	Adv. s. stress impact/TA	SRISK stress impact/Mcap.	Adv. s. stress impact/Mcap.	SRISK impact/Adv. s. impact
Dexia	222,936	0.02	0.01	2.62	27.32	7,402.3	0.00
Österreichische VB	20,904	2.39	0.13	5.59	10.15	423.2	0.02
Hellenic Bank	6,384	0.32	0.11	4.07	14.28	534.8	0.03
Bank of Cyprus	30,342	1.31	0.21	4.58	16.55	359.8	0.05
Banca Monte dei Paschi	198,461	1.03	0.49	2.88	46.89	275.9	0.17
Eurobank Ergasias	77,586	3.96	1.71	7.07	42.81	177.2	0.24
IKB Deutsche Industriebank	27,617	1.46	0.39	1.46	26.22	98.6	0.27
Banca Carige	42,156	2.31	1.05	3.88	39.36	145.9	0.27
Permanent TSB Group	37,601	4.65	1.61	5.35	35.94	119.7	0.30
Banco Comercial Português	82,007	4.02	1.84	4.04	45.37	99.7	0.46
Banca Popolare di Milano	49,353	3.09	1.44	2.57	48.29	86.2	0.56
Banco BPI	42,700	4.05	1.30	1.93	30.33	45.2	0.67
Banca popolare dell'Emilia	61,758	3.99	1.64	2.21	43.22	58.4	0.74
Banca Popolare di Sondrio	32,770	4.06	1.73	2.28	43.26	57.2	0.76
Banco Popolare	126,043	2.03	1.06	1.34	53.79	67.9	0.79
National Bank of Greece	110,930	8.29	3.43	4.13	40.08	48.2	0.83
UBI Banca	124,242	3.82	1.56	1.85	43.10	50.9	0.85
Crédit Agricole Group	1,688,541	1.36	0.71	0.73	43.96	45.3	0.97
Commerzbank	549,654	2.34	1.12	1.11	46.64	46.0	1.01
Alpha Bank	73,697	9.67	4.29	4.20	45.23	44.3	1.02
Deutsche Bank AG	1,611,400	2.04	1.05	1.02	46.36	44.8	1.04
OP-Pohjola Group	100,991	10.29	2.27	2.00	42.58	37.4	1.14

Piraeus Bank	92,010	8.64	4.36	3.62	51.11	42.5	1.20
UniCredit	827,538	3.74	1.86	1.34	49.98	36.1	1.39
Intesa Sanpaolo	624,179	4.80	2.72	1.80	49.37	32.6	1.51
Aareal Bank	42,981	4.12	2.31	1.41	56.79	34.6	1.64
Banco Popular Español	146,709	5.58	2.62	1.43	45.75	25.0	1.83
Banco de Sabadell	163,441	4.63	1.82	0.96	38.24	20.1	1.90
Société Générale	1,214,193	2.78	1.46	0.76	48.87	25.4	1.92
BNP Paribas	1,810,522	4.05	2.02	0.93	46.50	21.4	2.17
KBC Group	238,686	6.92	3.68	1.69	51.01	23.5	2.17
Mediobanca	75,285	7.40	3.24	1.44	44.35	19.8	2.24
Credito Emiliano	31,531	6.42	2.62	1.13	37.83	16.3	2.32
Erste Group Bank	200,118	5.45	2.98	1.24	53.44	22.2	2.41
Bank of Ireland	132,133	6.40	2.78	1.15	40.55	16.8	2.42
Banco Santander	1,115,637	6.33	3.03	0.68	45.38	10.1	4.49
BBVA	582,575	8.61	4.19	0.93	46.91	10.4	4.52
ING Bank	787,644	3.54	2.58	0.54	51.66	10.9	4.74
Caja de Ahorros Barcelona	351,269	5.67	2.63	0.50	46.43	8.9	5.22
Allied Irish Banks	117,734	35.97	21.13	3.99	42.09	7.9	5.30
Bankinter	55,136	7.72	3.22	0.38	38.73	4.6	8.44
Nordea Bank Finland	304,761	6.34	6.05	0.64	45.93	4.9	9.42
HSBC Bank Malta	5,722	12.61	2.15	0.06	14.36	0.4	36.88

Total assets and market capitalisation are in million EUR. Market leverage ratio and stress impacts are reported in per cent. SRISK impact/Adv. scen. impact is the ratio of the SRISK stress impact over the adverse scenario stress impact. Banks are sorted according to this ratio. At the top of the table are banks that lose very little value in the SRISK stress scenario compared to the value they are expected to lose in the adverse stress scenario of the ECB stress test. At the bottom of the table are banks that suffer large losses under in the SRISK stress scenario relative to their losses in the adverse scenario of the ECB stress test.

with higher stress impact, while in the specifications scaled by total assets the effect of book leverage ratio was insignificant or negative.

Throughout the analysis we focused on the adverse scenario stress impact of the ECB/EBA stress test. We perform the same regressions with the baseline scenario stress impact as the dependent variables. The results are very similar but the significance levels of estimated coefficients and R^2 ratios are lower compared to the regressions for the adverse scenario, which is expected given that the variation of the stress impact across banks is lower in the baseline scenario. Furthermore, we verify whether the assumption that the error terms only display correlation within the country clusters critically affects the inference. The results show that this is not the case in general: our conclusion about statistical significance remains valid for the vast majority of the coefficients.

7.7 Conclusions

A number of policy papers by Acharya and Steffen (2014a,b) that raise doubt on robustness of the ECB stress test, using SRISK as a benchmark, motivate a deeper analysis of the way stress is modelled in order to assess which results are credible. Accounting for size reveals that the stress impact on bank capital implied by SRISK is only marginally correlated with the stress impact as modelled for the ECB/EBA stress test, and key components thereof such as credit losses and trading losses.

The fundamental differences in the construction of SRISK stress impact and ECB/EBA stress test impact are reflected in the results of the multivariate regression analysis. On the one hand, the ECB/EBA stress test impact, and in particular the losses in the banking book, can be understood in terms of risk factors associated with credit losses. They also can be explained by market-based measures of bank vulnerability such as CDS spreads, while trading book losses display a more idiosyncratic behaviour, after controlling for the proportion of trading book assets in total assets.

SRISK stress impact, on the other hand, is rather disconnected from both basic risk factors related to credit losses and market-implied measures of bank vulnerability.[13] It seems implausible that bank losses

---

[13] While public backstops and gambling on bail-out participation of debt holders could explain this to a certain extent, it would nevertheless be brave to argue that CDS spreads are therefore not informative.

in a stress scenario are unrelated to existing default frequencies in the corporate sector, impaired loan ratios, etc., even on the six-month horizon of the SRISK stress. While the turmoil of 2008 illustrated how banks can be brought into jeopardy not by the original credit losses but also by secondary exacerbating factors such as illiquidity spirals and fire sales, the impact of credit losses on bank risk cannot be negated. While our analysis can neither verify the results obtained by the ECB/EBA stress test nor the SRISK results, it facilitates an intuitive understanding of the main drivers behind the results.

SRISK stress impact is highly positively correlated with market leverage ratio, and also with price to book ratio, with R^2 in univariate regressions reaching 90% and 50% respectively. In other words, banks with a high ratio of equity to total assets are proportionally hit harder by the stress. To a certain extent this could be explained by riskier asset portfolios, but certainly not linearly to the extent found in the data. Furthermore, there is no reason why banks with a higher price-to-book ratio should suffer larger losses.

The findings suggest a rather mechanical relationship between SRISK stress impact and market leverage ratio, which can be explained by decomposing the analytical formula for SRISK stress impact appropriately. If heterogeneity in market leverage ratios is large, this is likely to dominate the heterogeneity in covariance of bank stock returns with the market index, and the market leverage becomes the driving factor behind the SRISK stress impact. This explains why SRISK and ECB stress test results diverge in particular for banks that are close to bankruptcy and banks that are extremely well capitalised.

The SRISK stress scenario is set up to model returns to equity holders; therefore the stress impact is bounded by the amount of equity. This is particularly worrying for banks that are initially insufficiently capitalised, where the limit on losses is most likely binding in a stress scenario. We show that this has severe practical implications; namely, the SRISK stress impact is lower than what the ECB stress test finds up to a factor of 270 for the least well capitalised bank.

While not denying the usefulness of market-implied measures of bank risk, we argue that the stress impact would have to be calculated relative to the total balance sheet. The difficulty in using a measure based on stock returns is to properly model losses in states where all equity is wiped out. The ECB/EBA stress test, on the other hand, models the entire asset side and thus captures the whole balance sheet; the challenges with this approach lie rather in the modelling of the stress scenario and losses of different asset classes.

References

Acharya, V., Engle, R. and Pierret, D. (2014). Testing macroprudential stress tests: The risk of regulatory risk weights. *Journal of Monetary Economics*, 65, 36–53.

Acharya, V., Engle, R. and Richardson, M. (2012). Capital shortfall: A new approach to ranking and regulating systemic risks. *American Economic Review*, 102(3), 59–64.

Acharya, V. and Steffen, S. (2014a). Benchmarking the European Central Bank's asset quality review and stress test: A tale of two leverage ratios. *VOX CEPR's Policy Portal*. Available at http://voxeu.org/article/benchmarking-aqr-tale-two-leverage-ratios

(2014b). Falling short of expectations? Stress-resting the European Banking System. *CEPS Policy Brief No. 315*. Brussels: Centre for European Policy Studies.

(2014c). Making sense of the comprehensive assessment. Working Paper, October 27. SAFE Policy Letter 32. Frankfurt: Research Center SAFE - Sustainable Architecture for Finance in Europe, Goethe University Frankfurt.

Alfaro, R. and Drehmann, M. (2009). Macro stress tests and crises: What can we learn? *BIS Quarterly Review*, (December), 29–42.

Angrist, J. D. and Pischke, J.-S. (2009). *Mostly Harmless Econometrics: An Empiricist's Companion*. Princeton, NJ: Princeton University Press.

Asness, C. and Frazzini, A. (2013). The devil in HML's details. *Journal of Portfolio Management*, 39(4), 49–68.

Barth, J. R., Caprio, G. and Levine, R. (2012). The evolution and impact of bank regulations. World Bank Policy Research Working Paper 6288, 1–27. Washington, DC: World Bank.

(2013). Bank regulation and supervision in 180 countries from 1999 to 2011. *Journal of Financial Economic Policy*, 5(2), 111–219.

Borio, C., Drehmann, M. and Tsatsaronis, K. (2014). Stress-testing macro stress testing: Does it live up to expectations? *Journal of Financial Stability*, 12 (December 2011), 3–15.

Cameron, A.C. and Miller, D. L. (2013). A practitioner's guide to cluster-robust inference. *Journal of Human Resources*, 50(2),317–372.

Carhart, M. M. (1997). On persistence in mutual fund performance. *Journal of Finance*, LII(1), 57–82.

ECB. (2014). Aggregate report on the Comprehensive Assessment. Frankfurt: European Central Bank, October 20.

ESRB. (2014). EBA/SSM stress test: The macroeconomic adverse scenario. (17 April), 1–17. Frankfurt: European Systemic Risk Board.

Fama, E. F. and French, K. R. (1993). Common risk factors in the returns on stocks and bonds. *Journal of Financial Economics*, 33(1), 3–56.

Garcia, R.I., Ibrahim, J.G. and Zhu, H. (2010). Variable selection for regression models with missing data. *Statistica Sinica*, 20(1), 149–165.

Kearns, A. (2004). Loan losses and the macroeconomy: A framework for stress testing credit institutions' financial well-being. *Financial Stability Report*, 111–122.

Mileris, R. (2012). Macroeconomic determinants of loan portfolio credit risk in banks. *Inzinerine Ekonomika-Engineering Economics*, 23(5), 496–504.

Pesaran, M. H., Schuermann, T., Treutler, B. et al. (2006). Macroeconomic Dynamics and Credit Risk: A Global Perspective. *Journal of Money Credit and Banking*, 38(5), 1211–1261.

Steffen, S. (2014). Robustness, validity and significance of the ECB's asset quality review and stress test exercise. *Study requested by the European Parliament's Economic and Monetary Affairs Committee*, 1–40.

Zou, H. (2006). The adaptive Lasso and its oracle properties. *Journal of the American Statistical Association*, 101(476), 1418–1429.

Appendix 7.1: Weighting Scheme

We use data on bank exposures to sixty-seven different countries to weight variables describing macroeconomic conditions. These data are from ECB and have a few limitations that need to be addressed. First, total exposures are not always equal to total assets. However, in most cases, more than 90% of assets are covered. Second, data on some exposures are missing for thirty banks in the AQR sample. We scale up other exposures of these banks so that they sum up to 100% of total assets. Then we assume that the banks, for which exposure data are missing completely, are exposed only to the country they are head-quartered in. Given that the covered banks have an average exposure of 73% to their home country, this is a reasonable approximation. Lastly, macroeconomic data are not available for all countries banks can have exposures to. We deal with this problem as follows. If, for example, government bond yield data for Luxembourg is missing, for the specific purpose of calculating the weighted government bond yield, the exposure of all banks towards Luxembourg is dropped and the remaining exposures are scaled up to sum to 100%. However, this procedure is applied only if the macroeconomic variable is available for the country the financial institution is headquartered in. If not, the macroeconomic variable is treated as missing for such a bank.

Appendix 7.2: Regression Setup

Variable selection is based on economic intuition, considering both the data availability of each variable and potential multi-collinearity. Therefore we show regression setups that achieve a coverage of around 105 banks, and the setups where the market based regressors are used, with a much lower coverage of around 40–50 banks. Multi-collinearity is an issue when too many variables relating to the macroeconomic environment are used, because the variation of these variables exists mainly on a country level (even though for some of the variables, owing to the weighting scheme linked to banks' exposures, there is some additional bank heterogeneity). Given that we cover banks in twelve countries, this limits the number of macrovariables that potentially do not display multi-collinearity to a maximum of eleven; in reality, because macrovariables are also correlated, the number of them that can be used simultaneously is much lower.

Using variable selection techniques such as least angle regressions or LASSO (Zou 2006) starting from the entire set of regressors is not adding much value, because of missing data for some regressors.[14] It is easier to control for this variation in sample size manually than inducing an algorithm to choose a setup where as many banks as possible remain in the sample. Also, applying an algorithm to groups of regressors with similar coverage undermines the whole idea of having a variable selection algorithm.

The cross-sectional regression analysis is performed via OLS but we rely on cluster robust standard errors. Note that this does not affect the parameter estimates. The choice of clusters takes into account the guidance from the literature (Angrist and Pischke 2009; Cameron and Miller 2013). Given that our macrovariables refer to baseline forecasts or past values and therefore do not reflect a stress scenario, the errors in the regressions are likely to be correlated across banks in the same country/region. Likewise it could be that we neglect bank characteristics that could be related to (1) size or (2) the business model, which would lead to errors being correlated across banks of similar size or a similar business model. Hence, ideally all these components should be reflected by the clusters, but given that we do not have sufficient observations to allow clustering along those three dimensions, we conduct a robustness analysis clustering by each of those three concepts separately.

The preferred setup is with clustering according to countries (twelve countries; results shown in the main text). This follows practice of other papers, in the context of regressions involving individual bank data this is done, for instance, in Barth, Caprio and Levine (2013).

Clustering according to the business model classification (nine categories[15]) also has strong economic appeal, while clustering by size suffers from the defect that bank size does not cluster well, but is rather a continuum of values that is artificially broken up into clusters. Furthermore, size is to a certain extent reflected in the business model classification, when it meaningfully supports clustering. For the

---

[14] Recent developments in variable selection algorithms include ways to overcome the problem of missing data, as discussed in Garcia, Ibrahim and Zhu (2010). The adaptive LASSO (Zou 2006) would be one way to deal with the missing data, and we intend to complement our setups by the preferred adaptive LASSO solution once this algorithm is implemented in STATA.

[15] Heinrich Kick (2015), mimeo, European Central Bank, Frankfurt.

robustness check we create clusters according to the following limits on the bank's total asset: Cluster 1: Size > EUR 800 bn, Cluster 2: EUR 40 bn–EUR 800 bn and Cluster 3: Size < EUR 40 bn. Due to the low number of clusters the variance of these standard errors is likely much larger than in the other specifications, but this clustering separates the global systemically important banks (G-SIBs) and the very small banks from the other banks and therefore has some economic motivation.

Since the number of clusters in each of our methods is rather small, calculating the cluster-robust standard errors increases the variance of the error estimates at the same time as reducing the bias. A priori, it is unknown which of these factors is more relevant in reality. We also cross-check the standard errors with Huber–White heteroscedasticity robust standard errors, which do not correct for intracluster correlation of the residuals. The main conclusion from this robustness analysis is that significance levels based on standard errors clustered by business model or bank size do not deviate strongly from those clustered by country; they actually result in tighter error bands for some parameters and wider error bands for other parameters without strongly impacting significance of the parameters values. The results based on Huber–White standard errors are also very similar. The main variables we interpret remain statistically significant.

8 | The Role of Personality in Financial Decisions and Financial Crises

THOMAS NOE AND NIR VULKAN

Personality traits such as being "aggressive" are actively frequently listed as job qualifications in the finance industry (Endlich 2000). Traders are commonly believed to have a "Wall Street personality." One of the causes attributed to the last financial crisis was the aggressive risk taking of traders and bankers. Some of this risk taking can no doubt be linked with compensation structures. However, it seems reasonable to consider whether the personalities of financial agents also played a role in the crisis.

Because preventing the next crisis is even more important than understanding the last, if personality is an important determinant of the behavior of actors in the financial sector, the economics profession has an even more important task – to provide policymakers and firms with tools they need to assess the effects of personality on aggregate economic outcomes. This requires building financial models that aggregate the effects of personality on individual actors and map these effects into economic models. In short, economist will need develop economic models that incorporate personality.

In the chapter, we show that, although the evidence produced thus far is limited, it all points in one direction: personality has a significant independent effect on the decisions of economic actors. Thus, economic modeling should incorporate personality variables. However, personality research has been developed primarily within social psychology. The social psychology perspective on decision making is fundamentally different from the economic and financial economics perspective. Thus, incorporation of personality into economics will be challenging. We lay out the issues involved and offer some tentative suggestions for surmounting the obstacles to developing "personality aware" models of financial behavior.

In the social-psychology literature, personality traits are defined as dispositional attributes of agents: attributes that reflect the inherent traits of agents rather than their responses to transitory stimuli from the agents' environment. So, for example, everyone sometimes acts aggressively but everyone does not have an aggressive disposition.

As we discuss in detail in the text that follows, personality traits are stable over time, measurable with well-established instruments, and appear to be substantially heritable. In short, they represent a nearly perfect sort of exogenous variation among agents. In this respect, personality traits contrast sharply with preference traits such as risk aversion, typically posited in economic models. Measurements of preference traits such as risk aversion are unstable and context dependent (Reynaud and Couture 2012). In fact, frequently subject risk preferences cannot be measured at all because subject responses to survey instruments are frequently inconsistent.

Moreover, social-psychology research has established that these traits have considerable explanatory power for predicting behavior in general. Thus, it is not surprising that firms, recruiting agencies, and hiring consultants make extensive use of personality measurement when making employment decisions. For example, ghSMART is a consulting firm that advises many leading corporations, venture capital firms, and hedge funds on the suitability of candidates for top executive positions. The personalities of job candidates referred to ghSMART are assessed through four-hour structured interviews that result in a twenty- to forty-page assessment (Kaplan and Sorensen 2016). The fact that firms are willing to pay for this sort of very expensive personality assessment seems to indicate that they believe that personality has significant predictive power for future executive performance.

Despite this academic evidence from social psychology and the wholesale adoption of personality trait measurement in the finance industry, financial economics research has devoted little attention to the effect of personality traits on financial decision making. In the discussion that follows we explain this apparent paradox. First, in Section 8.1 we develop the definition of personality trait employed in social psychology and present some of the evidence for the effect of personality on behavior. In Section 8.2 we consider in detail research on the effects of personality in economic and financial contexts. In Section 8.3 we consider possible approaches to fitting the personality model into economic models of decision making. Finally in Section 8.4 we consider these approaches in light of the evidence produced thus far on the effects of personality and suggest some possible approaches while, tentatively, ruling out some others.

8.1 Personality

Allport (1937, 1961) defines personality as the dynamic organization of characteristics that creates a person's cognitions, motivation, and behavior. Over the years, the study of personality psychology and individual differences encompassed many theoretical approaches. Arguably the most important approach is the trait (disposition) approach. Trait approaches assume that personality traits differ across individuals, but are stable within an individual (during adulthood) and over time (McCrae and Costa, 2003) and that these traits shape the person's behavior.[1]

The Five-Factor personality (FFM) Model (Costa and McCrae 1992; Goldberg 1993) (also known as the "Big 5" model) is the prominent trait-disposition theory of personality. According to this model, there are five major personality dimensions (or domains): Neuroticism, Extroversion, Conscientiousness, Agreeableness, and Openness to Experience. Each of these dimensions is further composed of several different facets. The Big 5 model is empirically based, and the five factors as well as their facets have been derived using factor analysis.[2]

Psychological research accumulated a great deal of evidence regarding traits and specific behaviors. Given our focus on risk-taking behavior by financial agents, the most relevant traits are those associated with risk taking. Risk taking is most associated with one of the Big Five traits: Neuroticism. Neuroticism, also defined as low emotional stability (Goldberg 1993), is characterized by a tendency to experience negative affectivity and psychological distress. Neurotic individuals are "ineffective in their attempts to cope with stress and are prone to engage in irrational thought" (Bettencourt et al. 2006, 754). They are more likely to experience anxiety, anger, guilt, and depression, and interpret ordinary situations as threatening (Matthews et al. 1998). The facets of neuroticism include anxiety, angry hostility, depression, self-consciousness, and impulsiveness. The facet of neuroticism most closely connected

[1] Examples can be found in Barrick and Mount (1991), Hogan and Holland (2003), Hurtz and Donovan (2000), Mount et al. (1994), Poropat (2009), Roberts et al. (2007); but see Morgeson et al. (2007) for a different perspective.
[2] In fact, most of the criticism of the Big 5 model revolves around the fact that the model is data driven rather than theory driven. See, for example, the comprehensive review by Block (2010).

with risk-taking is aggressiveness (angry hostility).[3] Aggressiveness is intended to increase social dominance, and cause pain or harm to others (Ferguson and Beaver 2009) and is associated with behaviors such as risk taking (Lerner and Keltner 2001).[4]

Bettencourt et al. (2006) present a meta-analytic review of personality and aggressive behavior. They conclude that personality should be included as a central variable in models of aggressive behavior. Marshall and Brown (2006) demonstrate that people who score higher on the aggressiveness trait are more reactive to provocation, resulting in more aggressive behavior. In a more related study, Lauriola and Levin (2001) demonstrate that individuals who score high in Neuroticism are more risk averse in the gains domain, but less risk averse in the losses domain.

8.2 The Effect of Personality on Economic and Financial Decisions

Little research has been performed on the effect of personality traits on economic and financial behavior. However, even this limited body of research has documented strong associations between personality and economic behavior. Mcinish (1982) measured the personality traits of sophisticated investors using a Rotter scale measuring "locus-of-control," the degree to which investors believe that their own (internal) actions affect their life outcomes versus outside (external) forces beyond their control. He found that high scores for an external locus of control were associated with higher portfolio risk measured using the capital asset pricing model (CAPM) beta.

In an experimental asset market composed of subject students, van Witteloostuijn and Muehlfeld (2007) documented a strong relationship between personality variables and trading behavior. Subjects who scored high on impatience and urgency exhibited higher trading frequencies, lower price sensitivity, and earned lower arbitrage profits.

[3] As opposed to antagonistic hostility that is associated with the (low) Agreeableness domain. We define aggressiveness as angry hostility rather than antagonistic hostility.

[4] We use the term anxiousness and aggressiveness to refer to the traits, while anxiety and aggression refer to states or behaviors.

Johnson, Rustichini, and MacDonald (2009) experimentally implemented a trust game in which, given trustworthy behavior by the trustee (agent being trusted), the trustor's (agent trusting) payoff is highest from trust *and* trustworthy behavior is a strictly dominant strategy for the trustee. The unique Nash equilibrium solution for this game is for the trustor to trust and the trustee to be trustworthy. However, in their experiment, a significant number of trustors did not trust. Johnson et al. (2009) found that this failure to trust even when trust is rational was strongly associated with a personality facet, alienation.

Rustichini et al. (2012) documented the statistical relationship between personality traits and a number of life outcomes related to risk taking – smoking, body mass index, credit score, job attachment, and truck accidents. They found that the explanatory power of personality variables is at least as great as the explanatory power of standard economic variables (e.g., risk aversion) and that, in some cases, personality variables have more than double the explanatory power of economic variables.

Kugler, Neeman, and Vulkan (2014) investigated anxiousness and aggressiveness in an experiment implementing a two-player symmetric entry game, where each player can guarantee a certain payoff by staying out. The certain payoff is less than the payoff a player receives if she is the only player to enter but higher than the payoff if both players enter. Because the choice of an optimal strategy depends on the players' beliefs regarding the behavior of the other players, this experimental design permits identification not only of the effects of personality but also of the effects of agents' conjectures about the personalities of other agents. Kugler et al. (2014) found that (1) aggressive players entered significantly more often than nonaggressive players; (2) anxious players entered significantly less often than non-anxious players, and (3) players were less likely to enter when matched with aggressive players and more likely to enter when matched with anxious players. Thus, the subjects' behavior was significantly affected not only by their own personality traits but also by their beliefs about the personality traits of other players.

Kaplan and Sorensen (2016) examined personality data collected by a major consulting firm, ghSmart, that specializes in personality evaluations for senior executive candidates. They found that the personality traits of CEO and non-CEO candidates differ significantly. Moreover, non-CEO candidates with high scores in "CEO" personality traits were more likely to eventually receive CEO appointments than non-CEO candidates with lower scores.

In a recent paper (Noe and Vulkan 2016), we reported on an experiment performed on seasoned financial professionals. In the experiment, the participants received signals of the value of possible alternative investments to a market tracking portfolio. The signals were parameterized so that, under a standard Bayesian evaluation, the alternative investment was both riskier and on average less profitable than investing in the tracking portfolio. We found that, in an individual decision context, personality factors had no explanatory power for investment decisions. However, in a group context, the personality trait aggressiveness had a large and economically significant positive effect on the probability of investing in the alternative asset. Moreover, in the group setting, standard economic variables had no significant impact on group decision making, and aggressiveness was only weakly and *negatively* correlated with risk tolerance. In short, for individual decisions, standard economic variables predicted behavior fairly well and personality variables played no role. In group decisions, economic variables had no predictive power and a personality trait, aggressiveness, had significant predictive power.

8.3 Personality and Financial Economics Paradigm

The psychological literature focuses on individual behavior and decisions and, as such, is not directly applicable to the strategic situations (games) frequently encountered by financial decision makers. At the same time, it is not concerned with aggregation, determining the aggregate effects of individual choices on economic outcomes. Thus, in order to apply the insights from this literature into predictive theories of the effect of personality on economic behavior, it is necessary to incorporate them into a framework that does consider strategic interactions of economic agents and their aggregate effects – the financial economic paradigm.

To understand the issues associated with incorporating personality into the standard financial economics paradigm, it is necessary to review the essential aspects of this paradigm. We concentrate initially on the expected utility framework and later explain how cognitive biases can frequently be interpreted as distortions of either the probability weights or payoff function of the expected utility model.

Financial economics borrows its basic paradigm of human action from economics. In the economics paradigm, agents act to maximize their welfare conditioned on given preferences over outcomes. In general this perspective permits preferences to be defined over choice sets that encompass the goods the agent personally consumes, the consumption pattern of other agents, public goods, etc. (e.g., Fehr and Schmidt 1999). Moreover, a wide variety of preference structures have been analyzed, including even rather exotic preference structures (e.g., Fishburn 1990). However, the vast majority of financial economics research, and almost all research aimed at developing testable structural models of the pricing and demand for financial assets, has worked with a "fragment" of this theory and assumed that agents have preferences determined solely by their own random payoffs and that these preferences can be represented by a utility function that maps random prospects into numbers, with higher numbers representing more preferred prospects. Because this framework is borrowed from economics we will refer to it as the "economic framework" even though it is not representative of all economics research on agent choice.

To understand this framework, consider a financial decision in which the utility of an agent depends on a random prospect. To minimize the technical complexity of the analysis assume that the random prospect's realized payoff assumes one of x_i possible values. A utility function maps random prospects, X, into numbers. If the utility function represents the preferences of a financial decision maker faithfully, then the number assigned to the prospect X will be higher than the number assigned to Y if and only if the decision maker prefers X to Y. The financial decision maker's preferences are described by the expected utility model if for all random prospects, utility, U, is determined by

$$U(X) = \sum_{i}^{n} u(x_i) p_i,$$

where u is a utility-of-wealth function that maps the realized payoff of the prospect, x_i into a number and p_i is the probability that the decision maker assigns to $X = x_i$.

Thus, the utility of prospects is determined by preferences, measured by the utility of wealth function, u, and beliefs, measured by the decision maker's probability distribution over realizations of the random prospect, p. This probability distribution is based on a fixed prior probability but might be updated by information. Updating is governed by Bayes' rule.

Behavioral theories of decision making can frequently be interpreted as injecting "distortions" into preferences or belief structures defined by the expected utility paradigm. For example, under the most influential behavioral model of choice, prospect theory (Kahneman and Tversky 1979), decision-maker utility, which we represent by V, is given by

$$V(X) = \sum_{i}^{n} v(x_i)\pi(p_i),\qquad\qquad (8.1)$$

where v is a valuation function for realized payoffs that is convex below a reference point, which represents the decision maker's status quo wealth, and concave above the reference point. π is a probability weighting function that overweights small probabilities and underweights large probabilities. Although a decision maker whose utility is given by a prospect theory has preferences inconsistent with the axioms that imply expected utility maximization, formally, the prospect theory model is quite similar to the expected utility model: under both models, the decision maker has a payoff function representing preferences over realized outcomes, u in the expected utility framework and v in the prospect theory framework. Under both, the decision maker has beliefs that assign weights to these payoffs, the outcomes' probability, p, under expected utility and the weighted probability $\pi(p)$ under prospect theory. Under both, the utility of the agent is a weighted sum of the payoffs.

Of course, it is easy to posit structures of beliefs and payoffs under which the belief-weighted sum of payoffs determines the utility of decision makers. It is much harder to justify these strictures. Expected utility theory is justified by an axiomatic normative framework: a set of axioms is assumed to characterize rational choice over prospects. These axioms imply the expected utility representation.

Behavioral theories are justified by appeals to evidence from cognitive psychology. Cognitive psychology is ideally positioned to provide such evidence, as its focus is on how agents form beliefs and preferences and how these beliefs and preferences influence action. Thus, the output of cognitive psychology research is easy to input into justifications for behavioral models of decision making; behavioral biases

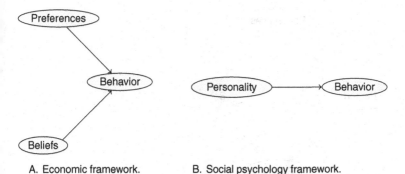

A. Economic framework.   B. Social psychology framework.

Figure 8.1 Frameworks for explaining economic behavior.

modify preferences and/or beliefs, and these modified preferences and beliefs determine agent actions. For this reason, it is not surprising that the behavioral biases identified by cognitive psychology have been readily adopted to produce economic models that incorporate loss aversion (Tversky and Kahneman 1991), overconfidence (Scheinkman and Xiong 2003), guilt (Battigalli and Dufwenberg 2007), and many other constructs from cognitive psychology.

Personality, however, falls in the domain of social psychology, and social psychology is not focused on preferences and beliefs. Rather, psychological research on personality focuses on the effect of dispositional attributes of decision makers, personality traits, on agent actions. Thus, as framed by the social psychology literature, personality factors are not an input into the model of preferences and beliefs. Rather, the social psychology framework "short-circuits" the economic model by positing a direct link between personality and the actions of decision makers. This difference in the conceptualization of the determinants of behavior between these two frameworks is illustrated in Figure 8.1.

Thus, incorporating the effects of personality on economic decisions is a much more challenging task than incorporating cognitive bases into the economic model. Two approaches to incorporation are fairly apparent: justify a causal relation between personality and one or both determinants of decisions in the economic framework – preferences and beliefs – or justify a "dual-self model" in which agents normally make decisions based on a utility function maximization of the type considered by rational choice and behavioral economics, but in some

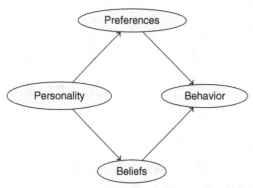

Figure 8.2. *Integration framework.* Personality effects are mediated through preferences and beliefs.

cases "personality takes over" and personality traits lead directly to decisions that are not rationalizable though agent utility functions.

The first approach to incorporation, which we term the *integration approach*, treats personality traits as inputs to formation of preference and/or beliefs. In contrast to the situation with cognitive psychology, integration does not simply require applying the results of the psychological literature to the economic variables. As discussed earlier, there has been little research linking personality directly to beliefs and preferences. Thus, empirical research is required to document the nature of such links.

In the integration framework, personality has a causal effect on beliefs and preferences. Beliefs and preferences then fix the behavior of decision makers. The causal structure of the integration approach is depicted in Figure 8.2.

Although significant, empirical evidence will be required to justify the sort of causal effects postulated by an integration approach, a priori there are many plausible justifications for causal relations between personality and preferences/beliefs. For example, aggressiveness has been linked to down-side risk taking. This evidence might be rationalized in the integration framework as resulting either from aggressiveness inducing utility-of-wealth functions that exhibit increasing absolute or relative risk aversion or by positing that aggressiveness leads to probability weighting functions that underweight the probability of losses. Note that the first alternative has personality acting on a rational-choice expected utility and the second on a behavioral objective function based on prospect theory. Thus, in principle, there is no logical impediment even to integrating personality into a nonbehavioral rational-choice paradigm of decision making.

Many other causal links are also plausible. Conscientiousness might increase risk aversion. Aggressiveness, in competitive situations, might lead to agent utility functions that weighed more heavily on the rank of the agents' payoff relative to other agents rather than the absolute magnitude of the payoff. Alternatively, aggressiveness might lead to overconfidence and thus an overweighting of the probabilities for upside payoffs.

The problem with the integration approach is not so much the lack of plausible hypotheses for causal relations but rather the lack of evidence to distinguish these hypotheses. Separating the effects of beliefs and preferences is a general and fairly intractable problem of identification in economics research.

Justification of the integration approach introduces an additional source of complexity: not only do the effects of beliefs and preferences have to be identified from observations of actions that are determined by both, but, in order to identify the causal mechanism through which personality acts, also the effect of personality must be "localized" to beliefs or preferences by the experimental design, i.e., by experiment structured so that personality will affect either beliefs or preferences but not both. For example, belief effects could be controlled through experiments involving complete information games. Such designs would fix beliefs and thus restrict personality to affecting preferences. These sorts of controls will require careful controlled experiments which are typically possible only in a laboratory setting.

The advantage of the integration approach is that it incorporates personality into a unified theory of financial decision making. In fact, in a formal theoretical sense, under the integration approach, the standard model would not change at all. Economics research typically takes preferences and beliefs as exogenous inputs from which, using maximization, either under a rational-choice or behavioral objective function, predictions about behavior are generated. Whether or not these "inputs" derive from personality or some other source is not relevant to predicting their effect on behavior conditioned on their effect on beliefs and preferences. Of course, when economic models are applied, identification of preferences and beliefs is required to derive determinant predictions of behavior. Personality,

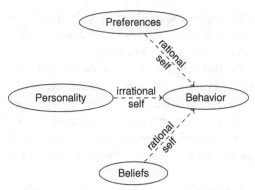

Figure 8.3 *Dual-self framework*. Depending on the context, the dispositional or rational self controls behavior.

if it explains a significant variation in preference and beliefs, would thus greatly facilitate the application of economic models to real-world problems.

In contrast, the second possible approach to incorporating personality into economic analysis is to use it to bound the scope of application for the economic framework. This approach is consistent with research positing that economic agents have multiple "selves" and that which self makes a particular economic decision depends on the decision's context (Peleg and Yaari 1973; Strotz 1955). Using this idea, the social psychology model and the economic model might share control agent behavior. Instead of a unified theory of decision making, this approach, which we term the *dual-self approach*, postulates two selves for economic agents a "calculating self" that makes utility maximizing choices using some consistent but perhaps behavioral utility function and a "dispositional self" that acts without calculation on the basis of personality traits. In some contexts, the dispositional self determines agent behavior, in others the rational self. The advantage of this approach is that it would not require integrating social psychology model of disposition and action into the economic model of utility maximization. The causal model that would underlie a dual-self formulation is presented in Figure 8.3.

The advantage of dual-self model is that it does not require integrating personality into the economic model. Instead, preferences and beliefs of the calculating self could be treated as exogenous and decisions produced by these beliefs and preference can be deduced from the standard economic calculus of optimization. Decisions produced by the dispositional self could be modeled simply as they are in social psychology, as primitive determinants of behavior.

However, this approach has a number of drawbacks that seem to outweigh this benefit. One obvious problem with the approach is determining when the calculating self as opposed to the dispositional self is controlling behavior. On this question, we have little insight, perhaps even less than we do for the potential effects of personality on preferences and beliefs. In addition, the dual-self approach would likely lead to models that predicted extreme shifts in agent behavior in response to small context changes. In a context that almost triggers the dispositional self, an agent behavior might be completely consistent with the axioms of expected utility. A small shift in the context that then triggered the dispositional self would result in large changes in behavior because personality traits, which do not affect the agents' calculating self, would now completely determine the agent's dispositional-self behavior.

Finally, some fundamental results in financial economics impose extremely weak demands on trader rationality. For example, contingent claim pricing models that derive the relation between the price of an asset and the price of claims written on the asset (e.g., an option on the asset) are founded on arbitrage principles – deviations from the predicted price relationship between the asset and the contingent claim permit trading strategies that sometimes generate gains over a fixed and finite time horizon, never generate losses, and require no commitment of capital. Although it is conceivable that some sort of triggering event might lead to a shift in control of trader behavior – the dispositional self – and thus lead to, say, a bubble in asset prices, it is hard to imagine that the triggering event would also lead to a "bubble" in the relative prices of assets and their contingent claims. No one has ever even advanced the idea that such relative price bubbles occur. Thus, to fit reality, a dual-self model would need to condition trigger events not only on psychological variables but also on economic characteristics of the trading environment. Thus, the social psychology framework would still in some sense have to be integrated with the economic framework at the level of triggering events. Overall, the dual-self approach appears to be a less promising approach than the integration approach.

8.4 Tentative Conclusions

From our discussion one can conclude that (1) personality variables have significant predictive power for predicting economic behavior, sometimes far more than the variables typically employed by economists and (2) these variables, being drawn from a different paradigm for human action, are difficult to integrate into the economic framework for decision making; and (3) integration is required if personality is going to be used in testable structural models of aggregate economic behavior.

Thus far, progress has been limited to (2). However, research provides some guidance about how integration might be accomplished. Most of the guidance, unfortunately, is of an exclusionary variety – casting doubt on simple routes to integration rather than identifying the best route.

Perhaps the simplest route to integration is to integrate personality into the classical expected utility framework. In this framework, beliefs are fixed by prior probabilities and Bayesian updating. Preferences are determined solely by monetary rewards from random prospects. Thus, personality could affect decisions only through changing risk preferences. However, our work and the work of others suggests that personality variables are only weakly correlated with standard measures of risk attitudes even when they have significant effects on behavior (Noe and Vulkan 2016; Rustichini et al. 2012). Thus, at least based on current evidence, it appears that the standard expected utility framework circumscribes the channels through which personality can act too much to permit the integration of personality into economic modeling.

Another somewhat more complex but nevertheless attractive approach would be to integrate personality into the belief formation process of agents whose decision calculus is affected by cognitive biases. However, our experimental results show that the effect of personality on decisions depends on social context of the decisions. We found that personality had a strong effect in group decision contexts and an insignificant effect in individual decision contexts. One would not expect that an agent's cognitive biases would vary based on the social context. Johnson et al. (2009) implement a game in which probabilities are specified by the experimenter and where all choices for the agents are so stark that the solution of the game is the same regardless of whether the agents are expected utility maximizers or maximizers of any standard behavioral utility function. Yet personality had a significant effect on players' actions. When choices are invariant with belief distortion, the effect of personality on beliefs should not affect outcomes. Thus, the evidence presented in Johnson et al. (2009) also seems inconsistent with personality affecting only beliefs.

Thus, although integration might require incorporating the effect of personality on cognitive biases, it will almost certainly require integration of personality into valuation functions. This will require incorporating into the model of financial decision making more factors than simple monetary payoffs.

On obvious candidate for incorporation is suggested by an obvious difference between decisions in group and individual contexts, which our work suggests has significant effects on the power of personality to shape behavior. When making decisions in a group context we care not only about the monetary rewards generated by the decision but also about our status, whether we "came out on top" or at least did not come out on the bottom. Recently, there has been a great deal of research in economics on status-based preferences and risk taking to attain status-based rewards (Fang and Noe 2016; Ray and Robson 2012). Thus we conjecture that a promising avenue for future research is measuring the effect of personality variables, particularly variables such as aggressiveness, which seems by its nature to involve status concerns, on the strength of agents' status-based preferences.

Of course, there is very little evidence thus far on the contextual dependence of the effect of personality on decision making. Hence, there may well be other more promising routes for augmenting the classical utility-of-wealth or behavioral payoff fiction to incorporate arguments that are sensitive to personality. At this point, the jury is still out. The effects of personality on economic decision making are an elusive prey but one that will be quite rewarding to capture. The gains from capture will accrue not only to economic science but also to society at large because economic models informed by personality will be better able to capture warning signs for looming financial crises and thus provide policymakers with the tools they require to avert them.

References

Allport, G. W. (1937). *Personality*. New York: Holt.
    (1961). *Pattern and Growth in Personality*. New York: Holt, Reinhart & Winston.

Barrick, M. R., and Mount, M. K. (1991). The big five personality dimensions and job performance: A meta-analysis. *Personnel Psychology* 44(1), 1–26.

Battigalli, P., and Dufwenberg, M. (2007). Guilt in games. *The American Economic Review*, 170–176.

Bettencourt, B., Talley, A., Benjamin, A. J., and Valentine, J. (2006). Personality and aggressive behavior under provoking and neutral conditions: A meta-analytic review. *Psychological Bulletin* 132(5), 751.

Block, J. (2010). The five-factor framing of personality and beyond: Some ruminations. *Psychological Inquiry* 21(1), 2–25.

Costa, P. T., and McCrae, R. R. (1992). Four ways five factors are basic. *Personality and Individual Differences* 13(6), 653–665.

Endlich, L. (2000). *Goldman Sachs: The Culture of Success.* New York: Simon and Schuster.

Fang, D., and Noe, T. H. (2016). Skewing the odds: Taking risks for rank-based rewards. Working Paper. Oxford: Saïd Business School.

Fehr, E., and Schmidt, K. M. (1999). A theory of fairness, competition, and cooperation. *Quarterly Journal of Economics* 114(3), 817–868.

Ferguson, C. J., and Beaver, K. M. (2009). Natural born killers: The genetic origins of extreme violence. *Aggression and Violent Behavior* 14(5), 286–294.

Fishburn, P. C. (1990). Additive non-transitive preferences. *Economics Letters* 34(4), 317–321.

Goldberg, L. R. (1993). The structure of phenotypic personality traits. *American Psychologist* 48(1), 26.

Hogan, J., and Holland, B. (2003). Using theory to evaluate personality and job-performance relations: A socioanalytic perspective. *Journal of Applied Psychology* 88(1), 100.

Hurtz, G. M., and Donovan, J. J. (2000). Personality and job performance: The big five revisited. *Journal of Applied Psychology* 85(6), 869.

Johnson, M. K., Rustichini, A., and MacDonald, A. W. (2009). Suspicious personality predicts behavior on a social decision-making task. *Personality and Individual Differences* 47(1), 30–35.

Kahneman, D., and Tversky, A. (1979). Prospect theory: An analysis of decision under risk. *Econometrica* 47, 263–291.

Kaplan, S., and Sorensen, M. (2016). Are CEOs different? Characteristics of top managers. Working Paper. Boston: Harvard Business School.

Kugler, T., Neeman, Z., and Vulkan, N. (2014). Personality traits and strategic behavior: Anxiousness and aggressiveness in entry games. *Journal of Economic Psychology* 42, 136–147.

Lauriola, M., and Levin, I. P. (2001). Personality traits and risky decision-making in a controlled experimental task: An exploratory study. *Personality and Individual Differences* 31(2), 215–226.

Lerner, J. S., and Keltner, D. (2001). Fear, anger, and risk. *Journal of Personality and Social Psychology* 81(1), 146.

Marshall, M. A., and Brown, J. D. (2006). Trait aggressiveness and situational provocation: A test of the traits as situational sensitivities (tass) model. *Personality and Social Psychology Bulletin* 32(8), 1100–1113.

Matthews, G., Saklofske, D. H., Costa Jr, P. T., Deary, I. J., and Zeidner, M. (1998). Dimensional models of personality: A framework for systematic clinical assessment. *European Journal of Psychological Assessment* 14(1), 36.

McCrae, R. R., and Costa, P. T. (2003). *Personality in Adulthood: A Five-Factor Theory Perspective.* New York: Guilford Press.

McInish, T. H. (1982). Individual investors and risk-taking. *Journal of Economic Psychology* 2(2), 125–136.

Morgeson, F. P., Campion, M. A., Dipboye, R. L., Hollenbeck, J. R., Murphy, K., and Schmitt, N. (2007). Are we getting fooled again? coming to terms with limitations in the use of personality tests for personnel selection. *Personnel Psychology* 60(4), 1029–1049.

Mount, M. K., Barrick, M. R., and Strauss, J. P. (1994). Validity of observer ratings of the big five personality factors. *Journal of Applied Psychology* 79(2), 272.

Noe, T., and Vulkan, N., (2016). Naked aggression. Working Paper. Oxford: Saïd Business School.

Peleg, B., and Yaari, M. E. (1973). On the existence of a consistent course of action when tastes are changing. *The Review of Economic Studies* 40(3), 391–401.

Poropat, A. E. (2009). A meta-analysis of the five-factor model of personality and academic performance. *Psychological bulletin* 135(2), 322.

Ray, D., and Robson, A. (2012). Status, intertemporal choice, and risk-taking. *Econometrica* 80(4), 1505–1531.

Reynaud, A., and Couture, S. (2012). Stability of risk preference measures: Results from a field experiment on French farmers. *Theory and Decision* 73(2), 203–221.

Roberts, B. W., Kuncel, N. R., Shiner, R., Caspi, A., and Goldberg, L. R. (2007). The power of personality: The comparative validity of personality traits, socioeconomic status, and cognitive ability for predicting important life outcomes. *Perspectives on Psychological Science* 2(4), 313–345.

Rustichini, A., DeYoung, C. G., Anderson, J. C., and Burks, S. V. (2012). Toward the integration of personality theory and decision theory in the explanation of economic and health behavior. IZA Discussion Paper. Bonn: IZA Institute of Labor Economics.

Scheinkman, J. A., and Xiong, W. (2003). Overconfidence and speculative bubbles. *Journal of Political Economy* 111(6), 1183–1220.

Strotz, R. H. (1955). Myopia and inconsistency in dynamic utility maximization. *The Review of Economic Studies* 23(3), 165–180.

Tversky, A., and Kahneman, D. (1991). Loss aversion in riskless choice: A reference-dependent model. *The Quarterly Journal of Economics* 106(4), 1039–1061.

van Witteloostuijn, A., and Muehlfeld, K. (2007). Trader personality and trading performance. Discussion Paper Series # nr: 08-28. Utrecht: Tjalling C. Koopmans Research Institute.

9 | *Model Apocalypto*

RADU TUNARU

9.1 Introduction

Finance was part of the evolution of humanity for thousands of years. Follow the money and you will understand the course of history. The nascency of mathematics was triggered by the need to solve problems related to money and finance. Modern finance experienced a meteoric rise in the 1980s, coupled with the introduction of computers on a large scale and also with the liberalisation of financial markets. Scientists from many other disciplines such as mathematics, statistics, physics, mechanics, engineering and economics, found a new uncharted territory in modern finance and they embraced the new 'gold' scientific race.

After a sunrise there is a sunset, and exuberance quite often masks the lack of a full understanding of the complexity of problems that may surface at any moment in time. The series of crises in finance culminated with the subprime-liquidity crisis that started[1] in 2007 that was reminiscent of the financial crash of 1929. Who was to blame and what really happened is still the subject of intensive research, and valuable lessons are to be learned.

While everybody is offering an opinion about toxic assets and liquidity measures and trying to design measures of systemic risk impact, not enough attention is paid, in my opinion, to another source of future problems that could also reach catastrophic and endemic levels – that is the risk carried by different models, or, in short, *model risk*. What is

[1] When has it ended?

Acknowledgements: I am grateful to Kevin James, Esa Jokivuolle, Adrian Pop and Michael Reilly for sharing their views on some parts of an earlier version of this chapter and to Chris Argyropoulos for some useful technical assistance. I am also in debt to the participants at the one-day workshop 'From the First Financial Crisis to the Next: Looking on the Horizon', September 2015 in Canterbury for insightful discussions. All remaining mistakes are obviously mine.

model risk? Is it important? Can we measure it? These questions are
very important for financial markets.

9.1.1 Is Model Risk Important?

There were already manifestations of model risk that led to substantial
losses, and it may sound cliché to say that these were only the tip of
the iceberg. In 1987 Merrill Lynch reported losses of 300 million USD
on stripped mortgage-backed securities because of an incorrect pricing
model and five years later in 1992 J.P. Morgan lost about 200 million
USD in the mortgage-backed securities market because of inadequate
modelling of prepayments. Bank of Tokyo/Mitsubishi announced in
March 1997 that its New York subsidiary dealing with derivatives
had incurred an 83 million USD loss because its internal pricing model
overvalued a portfolio of swaps and options on USD interest rates.
Dowd (2002) pointed out that the loss was caused by wrongly using a
one-factor Black–Derman–Toy (BDT) model to trade swaptions. The
model was calibrated to market prices of at-the-money (ATM) swaptions but used to trade out-of-the-money (OTM) Bermudan swaptions,
which was not appropriate. With the benefit of hindsight it is known
now that pricing OTM swaptions and Bermudan swaptions requires
multi-factor models. Also in 1997, NatWest Capital Markets reported
a £50 million loss because of a mispriced portfolio of German and
UK interest rate derivatives on the book of a single derivatives trader
in London who fed his own estimates of volatility into a model pricing OTC interest rate options with long maturities. The estimates
were high and led to fictitious profits. It is not clear whether the
trader simply inflated the volatility estimate or came up with the estimate that was more 'convenient' to him. Elliott (1997) pointed out
that these losses were directly linked to model risk. Williams (1999)
remarked that model risk was not included in standard risk management software, and in 1999 about 5 billion USD losses were caused
by model risk.

The recent advances of algorithmic trading add another dimension to model risk. It is difficult to say what exactly is happening
and who is to blame in this new type of superfast trading, most of
it being opaque and difficult to control. A Deutsche Bank subsidiary in Japan used some smart models to trade electronically that
went wild in June 2010, going into an infinite loop and taking out

a 183 billion USD stock position. In using computers, any mistakes are now executed thousands of times faster than before. There is no doubt in my mind that the next big financial crisis will be generated by model risk.

Model risk has been identified in all asset classes: see Gibson (2000) and Morini (2011) for interest rate products, Satchell and Christodoulakis (2008) and Rösch and Scheule (2010) for portfolio applications, Satchell and Christodoulakis (2008), Rösch and Scheule (2010) and Morini (2011) for credit products and Campolongo, Jönsson and Schoutens (2013) for asset-backed securities. It has also been recognised in relation to measuring market risk; see Figlewski (2004), Escanciano and Olmo (2010), Boucher et al. (2014) and Danielsson et al. (2014b).

The concepts of risk and uncertainty have been intertwined. In contrast to risk, uncertainty is a recognition of the existence of outcomes unspecified that may still occur and with which we do not have any way of associating a probability. Playing roulette falls in the first category; saying whether there is life on a faraway planet is an example of the latter and predicting the next type of fish you will encounter when going deep in the ocean is an example where both risk and uncertainty are combined. Likewise, we can make statements about the possible future value of the share price of Apple but we cannot say very much on the source of the next big crash in financial markets. Hence, the share price of Apple is risky while the source of the next big financial collapse is uncertain. The important distinction between risk and uncertainty goes back to Knight (1921), who pointed out that risk stems from situations in which we do not know the outcome of a scenario, but can accurately measure the probability of occurrence. In contrast, uncertainty appears when it is not possible to know all the information required to determine the scenario probabilities a priori.

With the nascency of modern finance in the 1960s and 1970s, model risk and uncertainty in general have preoccupied researchers in relation to various problems studied. Thus, early mentions of model risk and uncertainty in finance include Merton (1969); Derman (1996); Jorion (1996); Crouhy, Galai and Mark (1998) and Green and Figlewski (1999). Further notable contributions can be found in Cairns (2000); Brooks and Persand (2002); Charemza (2002); Hull and Suo (2002); Talay and Zheng (2002); Alexander (2003); Cont (2006), Kerkhof, Melenberg and Schumacher (2010) and Boucher et al. (2014). A recent monograph on the subject covering various examples is Tunaru (2015).

9.1.2 Definition of Model Risk

There are many definitions of model risk in the literature. Here are some of these, showing the wide perspective on model risk in the previous literature. Gibson et al. (1999) state that 'model risk results from the inappropriate specification of a theoretical model or the use of an appropriate model but in an inadequate framework or for the wrong purpose' while for McNeil, Frey and Embrechts (2005) model risk can be defined as 'the risk that a financial institution incurs losses because its risk-management models are misspecified or because some of the assumptions underlying these models are not met in practice'. For Barrieu and Scandolo (2014) 'the hazard of working with a potentially not well-suited model is referred to as model risk' and Boucher et al. (2014) define model risk as 'the uncertainty in risk forecasting arising from estimation error and the use of an incorrect model'.

Without engaging here in a debate over the subtle difference between model risk and model uncertainty, my view on model risk is that as soon as we use a model to represent a natural occurring phenomenon we introduce a degree of simplification that may be beneficial over some periods but detrimental in others. Therefore, model risk is the inability of the proposed mathematical statistical structure to reflect homogeneously over time the object under analysis. If a model *consistently* overestimates market risk or credit risk by, say, 5% then this is a great model because all we need to do is to adjust for the *time-invariant* factor of 5% and get a very accurate representation of risk. The problem in financial markets, as discussed recently by Danielsson et al. (2014b) and Danielsson et al. (2014a) is the opposite. There are plenty of models working extremely well during normal times that give very bad results in turbulent times. They argue that 'formal model-risk analysis should be a part of the regulatory design process'. Similar views were echoed by Brooks and Persand (2002) and Berkowitz and O'Brien (2002). Whether risk in financial markets is purely endogenous, as advocated[2] by Danielsson et al. (2009), remains to be seen. The

---

[2] It is argued that risk in financial markets is generated by 'interaction between market participants and their desire to bypass risk control systems. As risk

investment banks disregarded the AAA ratings given by rating agencies to structured investment vehicles (SIVs), well before 2007, and they asked for collateralisation of the over-the-counter (OTC) credit default swaps and collateralised debt obligation (CDO) deals. Hence, there is evidence that investment banks may be ahead of regulators in recognising new financial risk threads emerging. Perhaps the financial risk is a combination of both endogenous and exogenous risk.

Model risk has also been identified to some extent by the Basel Committee on Banking Supervision in the Basel II framework; see Basel (2011). Financial institutions ought to gauge their model risk. Furthermore, model validation is one component of the Pillar 1 for Minimum Capital Requirements and Pillar 2 for Supervisory Review Process. Unfortunately, in the Basel III framework [see Basel (2010)] it is stated that there are 'a number of qualitative criteria that banks would have to meet before they are permitted to use a models-based approach'. Hence, the 'Model validation and backtesting' guidelines, which focus mainly on counterparty credit risk management, allow qualitative or subjective decisions. For example, insurance or reinsurance companies can compute their solvency capital requirement using an internal risk model if it is approved by the supervisory authorities. This can be interpreted in many ways and it allows room for discretion, which may compound model risk rather than control it.

9.1.3 Model Risk versus Operational Risk

It is important to distinguish between model risk and operational risk, even if the latter has multiple facets and it may be bundled together with model risk by some financial operators. One important aspect of operational risk, that should not be considered part of model risk, is data input error. The Vancouver stock exchange started a new index initialised at the level of 1000.000 in 1982. However, less than two years later it was observed that the index was constantly decreasing to about 520 despite the exchange setting records in value and volume as described in the *Wall Street Journal* in 1983. Upon further investigations it was revealed that the index, which was updated after every transaction, was recalculated by removing the decimals after the third decimal instead of rounding off. Hence, the correct final value of

takers and regulators learn over time, the price dynamics change, further frustrating risk forecasting'.

1098.892 became the published value of 520. Although it was a computational error, this is an example of operational risk after all and not of model risk.

Another facet of operational risk is given by fiscal–legal updating. Sudden changes in law may expose a bank to great losses. In the United Kingdom a law on lower dividend tax credit was exploited by UBS in the 1990s. The law was changed in 1997 and caused many banks to suffer immediate losses, with UBS incurring huge losses. In general (see Gibson 2000), models used by banks simply ignore the impact of sudden fiscal change.

How should we extract valuable inference using statistical analysis of data, including big data? Ideally, one would have a randomised, double-blind, replicated, controlled experiment with a sufficiently large sample size testing a clear hypothesis that will lead to the exact conclusion. Unfortunately, finance is an *observational social* science and most of the characteristics observed in the foregoing simply do not apply. Hence, the degree of reliability on the inference extracted with statistical methods is decaying with the increase in the dimensionality of the variables under analysis and it depends on data.

9.2 A Simple Exercise

Consider that an investor would like to know, at one point in time, say, 30 January 2015, the volatility on a particular asset at a one-month or a two-week horizon, for either a pricing exercise such as European option pricing or some risk management calculation. For simplicity we consider here four assets that are representative for their asset classes: FTSE100 equity index, USDGBP foreign exchange rate, XAU gold rate and the crude oil price index. For each series all four prices, Open, Close, High, Low, are collected. We use daily data between 12 August 1992 and 30 January 2015, downloaded from Bloomberg. For this period data are available for all four subseries: Open, Close, High, Low.

In this section a battery of models for calculating the volatility is employed, covering a range of models from historical volatility to GARCH (Generalised AutoRegressive Conditional Heteroskedasticity) models and even implied volatility, for each subseries.

9.2.1 Realised Volatility

The volatility is considered, by definition, to be the annual standard deviation of the returns of the financial time series. When the volatility is calculated on the back of realised time series path, this volatility is called *realised volatility*. In Table 9.1 are reported the results of volatility estimation using several estimation methods based on historical data. We compare not only methods of estimation but also the same method of estimation using different data inputs. Clearly the gold rate XAU has the most consistent volatility estimates, followed by equity index UKX and then the exchange rate USDGBP. The crude oil price volatility estimates vary the most, perhaps not surprisingly for macroeconomists, but not quite in accordance with the interpretations of the graphs. Furthermore, there is a clear variation of volatility estimates in the data input subseries, with the volatility estimates given by the Open, Close, High and Low time series of data for all four assets being quite different. In addition, counterintuitively, the volatility estimate based on the HIGH series is smaller than the volatility estimate based on the LOW series. This confirms somehow the leverage effect[3] emphasised by Black (1976) in the sense that the volatility of an asset is negatively correlated with the returns of that asset.

Table 9.1 also contains the volatility estimates for more advanced methods[4] of estimating volatility using historical data. For reference, if $R_i = \ln\left(\dfrac{S_{i+1}}{S_i}\right)$ the Close to Close estimator of volatility based on a sample of n returns is

$$\sigma_{\text{Close}} = \sqrt{\frac{252}{n}\sum_{i=1}^{n}R_i^2} \tag{9.1}$$

[3] An increase in leverage may lead to an increase in stock volatility. Figlewski and Wang (2000) found a strong 'leverage effect' associated with falling stock prices, but also some contradictory effects suggesting that the 'leverage effect' is in reality a 'down market effect' that may have little direct connection to firm leverage. Hasanhodzic and Lo (2013) provided an example of all-equity-financed companies where the inverse relationship between price and volatility was very strong but without existence of leverage.

[4] A succinct and elegant review of all these methods is found in Bennet and Gil (2012)

Table 9.1 *Historical volatility estimation using daily data between*
12 August 1992 and 30 January 2015

Method	UKX	USDGBP	XAU	USCRWTIC
Full historical sample				
Open to Open	0.1476	0.0884	0.1493	0.3375
Close to Close	0.1816	0.0903	0.1639	0.3694
High to High	0.1706	0.0821	0.1516	0.3507
Low to Low	0.1816	0.0911	0.1647	0.3784
High to Low Parkinson	0.1607	0.0957	0.1633	0.2376
Garman Klass	0.1518	0.0978	0.1635	0.2075
Garman Klass modified by Yang and Zhang	0.1520	0.0996	0.1655	0.3174
Roger and Satchell	0.1518	0.0996	0.1628	0.2053
Yang and Zhang	0.1567	0.1001	0.1649	0.3270
Average of all the volatilities above	0.1591	0.0972	0.1640	0.2774
Last year historical sample				
Close to Close	0.1219	0.0573	0.1487	0.2937
High-Low Parkinson	0.1091	0.0557	0.1470	0.1493
Garman Klass	0.1038	0.0555	0.1465	0.1096
Garman Klass modified by Yang and Zhang	0.1036	0.0563	0.1464	0.2064
Roger and Satchell	0.1039	0.0550	0.1434	0.0922
Yang and Zhang	0.1067	0.0560	0.1442	0.2095
Average of all the volatilities above	0.1081	0.0560	0.1460	0.1768
Last two-year historical sample				
Close to Close	0.1212	0.0656	0.1870	0.2480
High Low Parkinson	0.1085	0.0642	0.1803	0.1252
Garman Klass	0.1031	0.0639	0.1781	0.0917
Garman Klass modified by Yang and Zhang	0.1030	0.0643	0.1779	0.1790
Roger and Satchell	0.1028	0.0631	0.1736	0.0764
Yang and Zhang	0.1058	0.0638	0.1756	0.1814
Average of all the volatilities above	0.1074	0.0642	0.1788	0.1503

Parkinson (1980) improved the estimation of volatility using extreme value theory statistical methods. Instead of logarithmic returns, this method works with the logarithmic ratios of High to Low prices, $\eta_i = \ln\left(\dfrac{H_i}{L_i}\right)$. The vol estimator is given by the formula

$$\sigma_{\text{High to Low}} = \sqrt{\frac{1}{4 \ln 2}\frac{252}{n}\sum_{i=1}^{n}\eta_i^2} \qquad (9.2)$$

Parkinson's estimator captures better the movements within the period, being more efficient than the Close to Close estimator, requiring five times fewer observations to be at the level of Close to Close estimator. Furthermore, Garman and Klass (1980) employed all four returns subseries and derived a vol estimator with an efficiency that requires seven times fewer observations in order to obtain the same statistical precision as the Close to Close estimator. The Garman Klass formula is

$$\sigma_{\text{HLOC}} = \sqrt{\frac{252}{n}\sum_{i=1}^{n}\left[\frac{1}{2}\left(\ln\frac{H_i}{L_i}\right)^2 - (2\ln 2 - 1)\left(\ln\frac{C_i}{O_i}\right)^2\right]} \qquad (9.3)$$

where C_i is the close price and O_i is the open price. This measure overlooks overnight jumps, so this estimator may underestimate volatility. The Rogers and Satchell (1991) vol estimator has the advantage that it can also handle securities with non-zero mean. Since it cannot account for opening jumps, this estimator may also underestimate the true volatility. The formula for this estimator with daily data is

$$\sigma_{\text{Rogers–Satchell}} = \sqrt{\frac{252}{n}\sum_{i=1}^{n}\ln\frac{H_i}{C_i}\ln\frac{H_i}{O_i} + \ln\frac{L_i}{C_i}\ln\frac{L_i}{O_i}} \qquad (9.4)$$

The Rogers–Satchell vol estimator can be up to eight more time efficient than the Close to Close estimator. An improvement on the Garman–Klass estimator was proposed by Yang and Zhang, who adjusted the estimator such that it will be able to handle opening jumps. The formula is

$$\sigma_{\text{GKYZ}} = \sqrt{\frac{252}{n}\sum_{i=1}^{n}\ln\left(\frac{O_i}{C_{i-1}}\right)^2 + \frac{1}{2}\left(\ln\frac{H_i}{L_i}\right)^2 - (2\ln(2)-1)\left(\ln\frac{C_i}{O_i}\right)^2} \qquad (9.5)$$

This estimator can also reach level of efficiency equal to eight. Yang and Zhang (2000) proposed also their own estimator capable of handling both opening jumps and non-zero drift. Their estimator can be fourteen times more efficient than the Close to Close estimator. The formulae for constructing this vol estimator with daily data are

$$\sigma_{\text{Yang–Zhang}} = \sqrt{252}\sqrt{\sigma_{\text{overnight}}^2 + k\sigma_{\text{open to close}}^2 + (1-k)\sigma_{\text{Rogers–Satchell}}^2} \qquad (9.6)$$

$$k = \frac{0.34}{1.34 + \dfrac{n+1}{n-1}} \qquad (9.7)$$

$$\sigma_{\text{overnight}}^2 = \frac{1}{n-1}\sum_{i=1}^{n}\left[\ln\left(\frac{O_i}{C_{i-1}}\right) - \overline{\ln\left(\frac{O_i}{C_{i-1}}\right)}\right]^2 \qquad (9.8)$$

$$\sigma_{\text{open to close}}^2 = \frac{1}{n-1}\sum_{i=1}^{n}\left[\ln\left(\frac{C_i}{O_i}\right) - \overline{\ln\left(\frac{C_i}{O_i}\right)}\right]^2 \qquad (9.9)$$

Note that $\overline{\ln\left(\frac{O_i}{C_{i-1}}\right)}$ denotes the sample average, likewise for $\overline{\ln\left(\frac{C_i}{O_i}\right)}$.

The estimation exercise is also repeated using only the most recent one year and two years of daily data, respectively. For equity, fx and gold a high degree of consistency is exhibited by the advanced historical methods. However, for crude oil price there is still wide variation across methods. Changing the sample reveals that historical volatility estimates may change vis-a-vis the full longer sample but also one year versus two years of data. Alarmingly, for USDGBP employing the last year of data led to a reduction in volatility from a 9.72% average for the full sample to only 5.60%, but using two years of data gave an estimate of 6.42%; while for XAU, the full sample average value of vol estimates was 16.40%, which changed to 14.60% based on only the previous year of historical data, and to 17.88% if the last two years of data were employed.[5]

[5] We can only hope that a market-maker is not trading options on gold with a volatility of 14.60% when he or she buys and with a volatility of 17.88% when he or she sells!

9.2.2. *Stochastic Volatility in Discrete Time*

Perhaps the problems highlighted in the previous section may be caused by the volatility clustering. GARCH models were proposed as a viable solution to this issue. Hence, several well-known GARCH models are estimated and employed to estimate the volatility of the four assets at the regulatory required horizon of two weeks. Once again the exercise is repeated for each subseries of prices. We compare the results obtained for GARCH(1,1), EGARCH(1,1), GJR(1,1) standard with a normal distribution, and also with a Student distribution in place of the normal distribution.

The results in Table 9.2 show the results for the equity index UKX, the foreign exchange USDGBP, gold price XAU and crude oil price USCRWTIC, for each subseries of sample data. Employing the GARCH(1,1) model[6], for UKX, the estimate based on the High prices *halves* the volatility when doing the same exercise with Open or Close series, while for USDGBP there is greater consistency across type of data series and models employed. It is somehow surprising that, under a given model, using the High series data gives a lower volatility estimate than using OPEN or CLOSE series.

Although at a first glance the gold rate is one of the most stable assets, the volatility estimation exercise illustrated in Table 9.2 suggests variation both horizontally and vertically. The same conclusion can be drawn for the crude oil. The same programs were used for all four assets classes simultaneously so the variation is even more puzzling. Note, for example, that the highest volatility forecasted for XAU was 0.00019 for EGARCH(1,1) models and the lowest was 0.0000765 obtained under the GARCH(1,1) with Student errors. In the same table we see that crude oil again has important variation both across models (vertically), as one would expect, but also across different data series (horizontally). A mischievous risk manager may use a GJR with a Student *t*-distribution and LOW series to report risk to investors while using a GARCH(1,1) with Gaussian innovations and CLOSE data series to price a financial product for a buyer. The relative difference is substantial, in the former case the two-week horizon daily volatility being estimated at 0.00035 while for the latter being calculated at 0.00120, an increase of 343%.

---

[6] There is ample evidence that this model fits well financial time series and likewise that is widely applied in financial markets.

Table 9.2 Two weeks ahead volatility estimate for FTSE100 (UKX), USDGBP foreign exchange, gold price XAU and crude oil price USCRWTIC using daily data between 12 August 1992 and 30 January 2015. All four subseries are used: Open, Close, High, Low

Method	UKX				USDGBP			
	Open	Close	High	Low	Open	Close	High	Low
GARCH(1,1)	0.00011	0.00010	5.8e-05	8.73e-05	2.46e-05	2.38e-05	2.38e-05	2.13e-05
EGARCH(1,1)	8.80e-05	9.76e-05	4.87e-05	7.59e-05	2.73e-05	2.58e-05	2.65e-05	2.35e-05
GJR(1,1)	9.53e-05	9.99e-05	4.65e-05	6.92e-05	2.61e-05	2.51e-05	2.29e-05	2.29e-05
GARCH(1,1)-t	9.16e-05	9.77e-05	6.37e-05	0.00010	3.75e-05	3.67e-05	2.41e-05	2.32e-05
EGARCH(1,1)-t	8.56e-05	9.57e-05	4.64e-05	7.42e-05	2.66e-05	2.52e-05	2.27e-05	2.20e-05
GJR(1,1)-t	9.64e-05	0.00010	5.59e-05	6.88e-05	2.67e-05	2.58e-05	2.32e-05	2.53e-05

Method	XAU				USCRWTIC			
	Open	Close	High	Low	Open	Close	High	Low
GARCH(1,1)	0.00014	0.00015	7.80e-05	0.00011	0.00051	0.00120	0.00075	0.00038
EGARCH(1,1)	0.00016	0.00019	8.43e-05	0.00012	0.00045	0.00071	0.00071	0.00045
GJR(1,1)	0.00015	0.00017	8.74e-05	0.00012	0.00051	0.00072	0.00072	0.00041
GARCH(1,1)-t	0.00014	0.00015	7.65e-05	0.00011	0.00051	0.00072	0.00072	0.00042
EGARCH(1,1)-t	0.00016	0.00019	9.03e-05	0.00013	0.00056	0.00069	0.00069	0.00049
GJR(1,1)-t	0.00015	0.00017	8.29e-05	0.00012	0.00057	0.00071	0.00070	0.00035

The results in both tables point out to several questions. What is the data time series that should be used for model estimation and forecast? How can we select the best models from several potentially good models? More importantly, are there any goodness-of-fit measures used to select the model or is this left to the devices of an analyst? Is it ok to change the subseries of data to feed the models? Should we expect models using distributions with fatter tails to produce larger volatility forecasts than models with distributions with 'normal' tails?

9.2.3 Calculating Risk Measures

Value-at-risk (VaR) is the most widely used measure of market risk. Since its proposal in 1996, thousands of papers have been published on how to improve VaR calculation. Here we compare VaR estimates obtained by four models– exponentially weighted moving average (EWMA), moving average (MA), historical simulation (HS) and GARCH(1,1) model, for all four asset classes and all four subseries of prices.

The exercise is carried out daily, using an estimation window of previous 600 observed data. The out-of-sample exercise covers the period 8 December 1994 to 30 January 2015, daily. A backtesting exercise is performed across asset classes, models and price series, giving a total of sixty-four different backtesting applications over the period 8 December 1994 to 30 January 2015, based on an out-of-sample VaR forecast. The results are presented in Table 9.3 and they suggest some interesting findings. Once again there is variation both horizontally across subseries of prices and also, as expected across models.

One might expect to see larger violation ratios when VaR calculations are based on the HIGH price subseries. While this is true for equity for all four models, it is not true for the other three asset classes USDGBP, XAU and USCRWTIC where violation ratios obtained under the LOW price series are larger. The GARCH model seems to be the most robust with respect to the independence test of backtesting. However, at the 99% confidence level, the GARCH(1,1) model for XAU has the opposite significance to the GARCH(1,1) model for UKX, USDGBP and USCRWTIC.

The backtesting results cannot pinpoint to a clear series of prices that has to be used and to a model that has to be employed, for the four major asset classes. While this is not entirely surprising given the

Table 9.3 *Backtesting results for VaR using exponentially weighted moving average (EWMA), moving average (MA), historical simulation (HS) and GARCH(1,1) model for FTSE100, USDGBP, gold price and crude oil price. The backtesting covers the period 8 December 1994 to 30 January 2015*

Method	UKX				USDGBP			
	Open	Close	High	Low	Open	Close	High	Low
Violation ratio								
EWMA	2.1046	2.0850	2.2227	2.4784	1.4242	1.5382	1.7660	2.1269
MA	2.498	2.4980	2.4784	2.5964	1.3103	1.2723	1.1014	1.8420
HS	1.3179	1.3965	1.4555	1.3572	0.9495	0.7976	0.9685	0.9305
GARCH(1,1)	1.6916	1.6522	1.967	2.2423	1.2913	1.3293	1.4432	1.7471
Bernoulli test								
EWMA	47.5561***	46.0549***	56.958***	79.5228***	8.4607***	13.2304***	25.4192***	51.0380***
MA	81.3762***	81.3762***	79.5228***	90.8831***	4.6658**	3.6316*	0.5295	30.2040***
HS	4.7172***	7.1884***	9.3432***	5.8940**	0.1380	2.3421	0.0534	0.2631
GARCH(1,1)	20.3404***	18.2574***	37.4591***	58.5893***	4.1338**	5.2272**	9.19***	24.2772***
Independence test								
EWMA	2.6262	2.7361*	0.7863	18.9761***	2.4341	0.3991	0.0754	2.3052
MA	15.5764***	15.5764***	22.2604***	50.3717***	5.9916**	3.3955*	0.1784	9.2756***
HS	6.1514**	5.4044**	11.4471***	21.7211***	6.2733**	3.9521**	2.6725	0.4947
GARCH(1,1)	0.1649	0.1240	1.6973	1.9296	0.0166	0.0052	0.6182	2.6365

Method	XAU				USCRWTIC			
	Open	Close	High	Low	Open	Close	High	Low
Violation ratio								
EWMA	2.1503	2.1694	1.8078	2.7973	2.0664	2.0465	1.8279	2.1061
MA	2.1123	2.0932	1.9981	2.6451	1.7683	1.9670	1.7683	1.9670
HS	1.1798	1.2369	1.2559	1.1418	0.9934	1.2915	1.1127	1.3113
GARCH(1,1)	1.9220	2.0172	1.6556	2.4548	1.6889	1.5100	1.5696	1.7683
Bernoulli test								
EWMA	52.8359***	54.3995***	27.9486***	115.2534***	44.2044***	42.7410***	27.9959***	47.1899***
MA	49.7630***	48.2541***	40.9916***	98.9576***	24.4271***	37.0876***	24.4271***	37.0876***
HS	1.6230	2.7707*	3.2162*	1.0202	0.0022	3.9554**	0.6225	4.4884**
GARCH(1,1)	35.5304***	42.4059***	19.0495***	79.9252***	19.9903***	11.4365***	14.0590***	24.4271***
Independence test								
EWMA	3.9410**	2.1016	0.8168	3.0874*	0.0111	0.3489	0.3344	1.1909
MA	2.3936	2.4959	10.3062***	18.4246***	7.6649***	21.7432***	14.1373***	29.8947***
HS	1.5390	3.6607*	6.5637**	7.8649***	2.6570	6.4866**	4.8835**	9.8081***
GARCH(1,1)	5.7627***	2.9309*	3.2070*	3.6758*	1.3523	0.5363	0.5202	0.2484

Note: '*', '**', and '***' indicates statistical significance at 10%, 5%, and 1%, respectively.

172   *Radu Tunaru*

different nature of the four assets investigated here, imagine how it is like in the real market where there are so many assets and dozens, if not hundreds, of models for calculating VaR.

9.3 Much Ado About Nothing?

9.3.1 A Lot

Modelling is seen by many as an art. The finance industry is driven by models, and real financial losses may occur due to wrong modelling. There is a quick list of tasks that anyone involved with models can follow in order to minimise his or her own wrongdoing.

1. Evaluate and verify the assumptions behind the model.
2. Test new models against well-known models and against known results.
3. Occam's razor principle. *Ceteris paribus*, the simpler model is always better.
4. Backtest and stress test your models against a wide range of scenarios using out-of-sample historical forecasts.
5. Understand the discrepancies and pitfalls of a given model without sweeping them under the carpet.
6. Re-calibrate and re-estimate your models periodically.

In my opinion there are far too many models in the financial literature and too little time is spent on fully understanding the intricacies of these models. Why should models on which important decisions are based and billions of dollars traded be validated in-house only? How many of these models will pass an independent review? If we do not dare to do similar things with new medicine why is it acceptable to do it with finance? Quantitative finance specialists are sometimes called rocket scientists because many physics researchers migrated into the field of finance. Would we board a rocket developed on the models an investment bank is using and let some of the traders give guidance from the control tower? A quant once said that a wrong statement cited four times becomes a theorem with a name. With recent advances in computer power, the same incorrect result is implemented and applied a thousand times faster.

A straightforward way to slow down the proliferation of models in finance is to ask investment banks, hedge funds and financial boutiques to pay royalties to the scientists who developed the models – one dollar, or even one cent, per transaction where the model has been used. Model creators will then be more diligent because there will be an incentive to take more time and design models that work better in a variety of circumstances, and are easy to explain, implement, calibrate and so on. Users will be inclined to scrutinise the models that they are using, as they will be paying for them. Further empirical comparative research is needed to backtest results across asset classes. Independent research and model validation can play a vital role in screening out models that carry deficiencies.

A very important role is supposed to be played by regulators. Who appoints the regulators and what qualifies a person to be a regulator? Actually the regulators are most of the time non-specialists and I believe that it is almost right that they are 'objective', in the sense that they need to see the forest, but have little knowledge about each tree. Model risk can be controlled only if we convince the market participants to be self-interested in sharing information and to proactively manage this type of risk. Regulators can passively manage model risk by facilitating debates and promoting best practice. Academics can work on both sides and can offer independent advice that should not be neglected. At the same time, are the textbooks in line with the latest market practices, regulations and product development? Quite often they are not and this is due to the fact that the innovation in financial markets is not always in the same space and time as academic research.

What if the regulators created a body to approve the models being used in the industry, model creators were paid an infinitesimal sum per transaction, bankers used the model they felt was most appropriate but documented how parameter estimates were arrived at and given specific inputs? Then model risk could be greatly reduced. The internet could facilitate this entire process in an elegant, productive and reliable manner.

9.3.2 A Little

Financial systems are complex. There are thousands of different financial instruments, financial regulations in different jurisdictions and millions of market participants world-wide. It is virtually impossible to have an accurate description and understanding of the dynamics of

174   *Radu Tunaru*

financial securities prices, second by second[7]. The only representation of this complex reality is via models. Models in finance are not like models in physics for a simple reason. The latter look at repeatable reality, the former do not because of human interactions. Hence, it is difficult to know whether modelling in finance should proceed from empirical to theoretical, as is done in physics, or from theoretical to empirical, as is done in biosciences. In my opinion, it is a combination of both, since finance neither has very clear theoretical rules as in biosciences nor can rely on homogeneous, repetitive data occurring at different points in time as in physics. Time itself contributes to changes in finance realities.

One thing is for certain. Finance is dependent on models, and as soon as we talk about models there is exposure to model risk. Hence, I am not suggesting and I cannot advocate total elimination of model risk because it simply cannot be done. What is important is realising and recognising that this risk does exist. Then, it is important to be critical at the model development stage, considering all aspects of modelling (how many models proposed in finance showed how to estimate those parameters?), and then periodically validate models looking at new datasets *and* old datasets, backtesting and stress-testing.

The evident and strong, but still esoteric, connection between regulators and market participants may cause distortions to any prescribed quantitative based risk management policy. In his famous public lecture at the Reserve Bank of Australia, Goodhart stated: 'Any statistical relationship will break down when used for policy purposes'. Danielsson (2002) followed up with a corollary saying that 'A risk model breaks down when used for regulatory purposes'. The main reason behind these statements is that as long as risk is modelled with behavioural equations that are assumed to be invariant under observation, the next financial crisis will always catch us on the wrong foot because it will be caused by new sources. Danielsson (2002) argued that since market data are endogenous to market behaviour, any statistical inference made from data covering periods of stability will not be helpful in times of crisis. Thus, from a financial stability point of view risk measures such as VaR or ES may potentially give misleading

[7] Algorithmic trading is considering activities taking place at millisecond frequencies.

information about risk, possibly even contributing indirectly to both idiosyncratic and systemic risk.

Since the effects of regulation on the risk and value of a company are important, is it possible to design regulations that do not themselves compromise the companies that form the financial markets? Brennan and Schwartz (1982) showed that it is possible to design a valuation model that takes into account the effects of the regulatory policy. However, there is still a long way to go to have a framework for regulation and model valuation and risk management that is integrated in a consistent manner at an industry level. There are educational barriers, incentive divergences and ultimately different risks faced by regulators, who are more interested in financial system stability overall; investors, who are more interested in returns for various levels of risk; and risk managers and auditors, who are interested in avoiding a repeat of previous crises.

Even when this theoretical argument is solved there is still something fundamental that is impossible to overcome: the difference between theoretical and empirical. Consider a set of conditions $C_1,...,C_m$ that must be satisfied by a risk measure in order for that risk measure to be unanimously accepted by academia, industry and regulatory bodies. Suppose that this measure ψ has been identified. For simplicity consider the situation of only two assets with risks X and Y and let us denote by $\psi(X,Y)\,|\,C_j$ the fact that the risk measure ψ satisfies condition C_j for any two financial risks X and Y.

Now consider $\tilde{X} = (X_1,...,X_n)$ and $\tilde{Y} = (Y_1,...,Y_n)$ two representative samples for the population unknown risks X and Y. It is obvious to me that we can have

$$\psi(X,Y)\,|\,C_j, \quad \forall j \in \{1,...,m\}$$

but there may exist $i \in \{1,...,m\}$ such that

$$\psi(\tilde{X},\tilde{Y}) \nmid C_i$$

In other words, a risk measure may satisfy all required *theoretical* properties but its *sampling* version may fail to satisfy all properties! As an example, VaR is subadditive under elliptical distributions, which include the Gaussian or normal distribution, but sampling error alone may invalidate this property for some given data.

9.4 Knowledge Production for Finance

In this section we discuss the production of 'knowledge' in finance, looking at volume and evolution of number of articles over years. The question here is the following: per year, how many new ideas, results and techniques should the staff working in a bank take into consideration? Without loss of generality we consider a large, top-tier, bank with both retail and investment arms, and with thousands of employees well qualified. Hence, there is no barrier of understanding new research when that is published. We assume that each paper contains at least ONE innovative idea or application that has not been done before.

The website gloriamundi.com accumulated by the summer of 2014 about 7,500 papers dedicated to financial risk management, covering hundreds of different models and methods to calculate Value at Risk (VaR), for example. This flurry of papers was very much the result of an effervescence in the 1990s. Nevertheless, this mountain of research could not stop the Enron disaster and the dotcom bubble of 2000s. The next chapter in financial evolution was in the 2000s with an explosion of research focused on credit risk, once the credit markets took off on the back of the credit default swap (CDS) concept. As of July 2014, more than 1,600 credit risk papers were available to download from www.defaultrisk.com, more than 250 of which were papers on credit risk models. Add to that the thousands of papers on derivatives pricing and hedging across various asset classes and you get the picture, a jungle.

Some may argue that one way to select the relevant research is to consider *only* the research published in peer reviewed journals. The graph in Figure 9.1 depicts the number of articles published between 1990 and 2014 by each journal rated 3* or better on the Association of Business Schools Academic Journal Guide 2015 list.

The number of papers published in each journal seems to have doubled over the last twenty-five years. The numbers represented in Figure 9.1 are *underestimating* the real number of new results and ideas published in several ways. First of all, only the journals classified in the field of finance were retained, but important results and techniques relevant to finance may be published in economics, statistics, mathematics or operations research journals. Second, only the

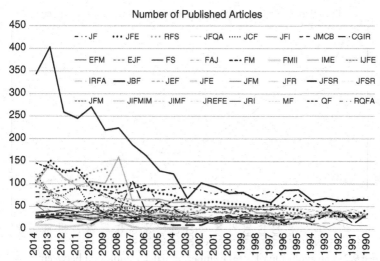

Figure 9.1 The evolution of number of articles published between 1990 and 2014 by each journal rated 3* or better on the Association of Business Schools Academic Journal Guide 2015 list.

Note: The following journals were excluded because they are very new, only few years in their existence: *Review of Finance* (formerly *European Finance Review*), *Annual Review of Financial Economics, Review of Asset Pricing Studies, Review of Corporate Finance Studies,* and *Financial Review*

journals rated in the ABS 2015 list at 3* or above are considered; the journals rated 2*, 1*, and even journals not rated by ABS, are not included.

The graph in Figure 9.2 illustrates the continuous growth of the total number of published journals in finance, from 428 in 1990 to a maximum of 2,339 in 2013 and 2,314 in 2014. This is an increase of more than fivefold in the last twenty-five years. As indicated on this graph, a linear trend will give a fit to this time-series with an $R^2 = 93\%$. A linear increase in production of knowledge in finance should be worrisome in terms of absorption. Unfortunately, we wished the production had a linear trend. In fact, as the graph in Figure 9.3 shows, an exponential trend is much closer to reality. If the exponential trend is some kind of long-run mean there is a clear indication of a reversion to the mean effect. What is coming as a total surprise is the years when the observed time-series of total number of published articles is reverting to the mean: 1994, 1996, 2002, 2008, 2012, 2013. The main

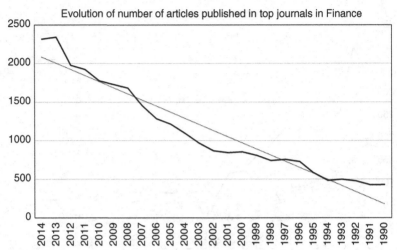

Figure 9.2 The evolution of total number of articles published between 1990 and 2014 in journals rated 3* or better on the Association of Business Schools Academic Journal Guide 2015 list. A linear trend has an $R^2 = 93\%$.

question here is for how long this trend can continue and, moreover, what would be a rational level for production of research articles in finance.

Conceptually the learning process has its roots in Bayes' updating formula

$$P(y \mid \text{research}) = \frac{P(\text{research} \mid y)}{P(\text{research})} P(y) \tag{9.10}$$

where y is a random variable quantifying the concept about which learning is sought such as the mean return of a stock, the standard deviation of a foreign exchange and so on, $P(y)$ is the prior probability reflecting the previous knowledge about y, $P(\text{research})$ is total research being carried out in general and $P(y \mid \text{research})$ is the updated learning after additional research is carried out. There are two ways to interpret Eq. (9.10). The first one is to regard research as the total research being carried out. Then, conditional on y, the total amount of research being carried out *less research on y that we know about* is still huge and the ratio $\dfrac{P(\text{research} \mid y)}{P(\text{research})} \approx 1$. In this case $P(y \mid \text{research}) \approx P(y)$, so huge amounts of research will not greatly improve knowledge

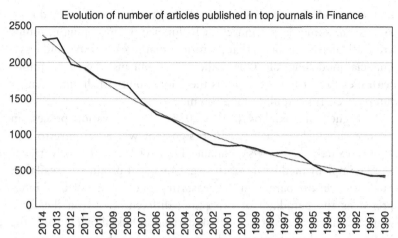

Figure 9.3 The evolution of total number of articles published between 1990 and 2014 in journals rated 3* or better on the Association of Business Schools Academic Journal Guide 2015 list. An exponential trend has an $R^2 = 98.58\%$.

about y itself. The second view is that research is carried out as starting from a root, with the assumption that no specific root means research on everything. Then $P(\text{research} \mid y)$ refers the research that is carried out only from what we already know about y. For any specific y this research will be very small compared to the total research pool and therefore $\dfrac{P(\text{research} \mid y)}{P(\text{research})} \approx 0$ when a very largeamount of information is generated in the learning process in general. Then $P(y \mid \text{research}) \approx 0 \times P(y) = 0$ so the effect on a particular concept y of the immense research unrelated to y is that it nullifies the prior knowledge one had on y. Either way, the exaggerated proliferation of research has a detrimental effect on individual topics.

Do we need an ever more mathematically sophisticated approach to finance? Soklakov (2013) argues masterfully that continuous-time finance operates mainly on changing drift via Girsanov operator while the markets are intrinsically constructed on volatility[8] trading. Furthermore, Soklakov (2013) argues that jumps were introduced in

---

[8] This great discrepancy is even more important because it is well known from a computational finance point of view that, for diffusion processes, it is very difficult to estimate drift while volatility can be more robustly estimated.

financial modelling to alleviate this discrepancy, although they do not arise from some deep connection to finance. In my opinion, jumps are mathematical gadgets that perform a mathematical role and less a financial modelling role. One of the main problems when using jumps with mean-reverting processes is the impossibility of disentangling a jump effect from a pull to long-run mean.

As argued in Soklakov (2010, 2013), the innovation process in finance should look at a payoff design that will allow investors to express exactly their views on financial markets. Complex skew trades can be implemented easily of the right financial product is available. Furthermore, the paradigm of measuring model risk can be reinterpreted as the paradigm of expressing different views on the same market. The measure of model risk derived in Soklakov (2013) is the Kullback–Leibler information divergence measure between the investor's subjective probability density and the market implied probability density on the same financial concept. Soklakov (2010) proposed a model design framework that makes a direct link between optimal payoff structures and likelihood functions. On the one hand it is reassuring that many results in mathematical statistics could be reinterpreted as tradable payoff structures. On the other hand, likelihood functions themselves may introduce various inconsistencies; see the examples discussed in Tunaru (2015).

9.5 Conclusion: Before Not Too Late

Recalling the 1986 presidential speech at the American Finance Association, Fisher Black said: 'In the end, a theory is accepted not because it is confirmed by conventional empirical tests, but because researchers persuade one another that the theory is correct and relevant.'

Convenience is often the enemy of progress. Researchers should try to criticise various models and techniques more. Only then can the models that survive the test of time be truly beneficial to us all.

There are many facets of model risk that require more intensive research. Alexander (2003) pointed out that firm-wide enterprise model risk will focus on the aggregated portfolio and therefore model validation that occurs at an individual risk level will not capture crude assumptions that are made with respect to dependencies, for example, at the aggregated level. Therefore, model risk must be dealt with at individual lines of business but also globally. Hence, one could argue that model validation in a bank should be carried out in a macroscopic as well as a microscopic manner.

In the aftermath of the subprime-liquidity crises there is a trend towards big-data analysis, hoping that more data and more analysis will alleviate, if not the occurrence, at least the severity of the future financial crises. As emphasised in Spiegelhalter (2014) this trend will lead to 'large n, really large p' problems, where n is the number of data observations and p is the number of parameters. Spiegelhalter (2014) points out that precision may be only illusory and various well-known statistical inference effects such as selection bias, regression to the mean, multiple testing and the eternal misinterpretation of associations as causation will lead to an exponential growth of false discoveries[9] if they are not taken into consideration by expert trained statisticians.

What is the model risk measure most valid theoretically *and* most useful practically? There are new frameworks being proposed but we need more involvement and debate before settling on a particular methodology. The linkage between hedging and model risk has not been investigated very much so far. Is it right to argue that hedging is a form of protection against model risk? Moreover, incomplete markets bring in a particular type of model risk, that is, model identification. Would it be right to select a suboptimal model that has a lower parameter estimation risk? Risk management has entered a new phase with direct implications for capital reserve calculations impacting on day-to-day operations. Should we also look at the 'good' risk, that is, the profit tail of the distribution? Questioning and debating more, and sharing openly more results can only improve taming model risk.

References

Alexander, C. (2003). The present and future of financial risk management. *Journal of Financial Econometrics* 3, 3–25.

Barrieu, P. and Scandolo, G. (2014). Assessing financial model risk. *European Journal of Operational Research* 242(2), 546–556.

Basel. (2010). Basel III: A global regulatory framework for more resilient banks and banking systems. Technical report, Basel Committee on Banking Supervision. Revised June 2011.

---

[9] It is still flabbergasting to see the number of articles published in finance journals where inference is based on regression models with R^2 less than 5%.

(2011). Revisions to the Basel II market risk framework. Technical report, Basel Committee on Banking Supervision.

Bennet, C. and Gil, M. (2012). Measuring historical volatility. Research market paper. Santander, Madrid, February, 2012.

Berkowitz, J. and O'Brien, J. (2002). How accurate are value-at-risk models at commercial banks?. *Journal of Finance* 57(3), 1093–1111.

Black, F. (1976). Studies of stock price volatility changes. In *Proceedings of the Business and Economics Section of the American Statistical Association*, 177–181. Alexandria, VA: American Statistical Association.

Boucher, C. M., Danielsson, J., Kouontchou, P. S. and Maillet, B. B. (2014). Risk models at risk. *Journal of Banking and Finance* 44, 72–92.

Brennan, M. and Schwartz, E. (1982). Consistent regulatory policy under uncertainty. *The Bell Journal of Economics* 13(2), 506–521.

Brooks, C. and Persand, G. (2002). Model choice and Value-at-Risk performance. *Financial Analysts Journal* 58(5), 87–97.

Cairns, A. J. (2000). A discussion of parameter and model uncertainty in insurance. *Insurance: Mathematics and Economics* 27, 313–330.

Campolongo, F., Jönsson, H. and Schoutens, W. (2013). *Quantitative Assessment of Securitisation Deals*. Springer Briefs in Finance. Heidelberg: Springer.

Charemza, W. (2002). Guesstimation. *Journal of Forecasting* 21, 417–433.

Cont, R. (2006). Model uncertainty and its impact on the pricing of derivative instruments. *Mathematical Finance* 13, 519–547.

Crouhy, M., Galai, D. and Mark, R. (1998). Model risk. *Journal of Financial Engineering* 7(3/4), 267–288.

Danielsson, J. (2002). The emperor has no clothes: Limits to risk modelling. *Journal of Banking and Finance* 26, 1273–1296.

Danielsson, J., James, K., Valenzuela, M. and Zer, I. (2014a). Model risk and the implications for risk management, macroprudential policy, and financial regulations. www.vox.eu.org.

(2014b). *Model Risk of Risk Models*. Finance and Economics Discussion Series 2014-34. Washington, DC: Federal Reserve Board.

Danielsson, J., Shin, H. S. and Zigrand, J.-P. (2009). Modelling financial turmoil through endogenous risk. www.vox.eu.org.

Derman, E. (1996). *Model Risk: Quantitative Strategies Research Notes*. New York: Goldman Sachs.

Dowd, K. (2002). *An Introduction to Market Risk Measurement*. Chichester: John Wiley & Sons.

Elliott, M. (1997). Controlling model risk. Derivatives Strategy. Available at www.DerivativesStrategy.com.

Escanciano, J. C. and Olmo, J. (2010). Backtesting parametric value-at-risk with estimation risk. *Journal of Business and Economic Statistics* 28(1), 36–51.

Figlewski, S. (2004). Estimation error in the assessment of financial risk exposure. Working Paper. New York: New York University.

Figlewski, S. and Wang, X. (2000). Is the leverage effect a leverage effect? Technical Report. New York and Hong Kong: NYU Stern School of Business and City University of Hong Kong.

Garman, M. and Klass, M. (1980). On the estimation of security price volatility from historical data. *Journal of Business* 53(1), 67–78.

Gibson, R., ed. (2000). *Model Risk: Concepts, Calibration and Pricing.* London: Risk Books.

Gibson, R., Lhabitant, F., Pistre, N. and Talay, D. (1999). Interest rate model risk: An overview.. *Journal of Risk* 3, 37–62.

Green, T. C. and Figlewski, S. (1999). Market risk and model risk for a financial institution writing options. *Journal of Finance* 54(4), 1465–1499.

Hasanhodzic, J. and Lo, A. W. (2013). Blacks leverage effect is not due to leverage. Working Paper. SSRN, www.ssrn.com/abstract=1762363.

Hull, J. C. and Suo, W. (2002). A methodology for assessing model risk and its application to the implied volatility function model. *Journal of Financial and Quantitative Analysis* 37(2), 297–318.

Jorion, P. (1996). Risk2: Measuring the risk in value-at-risk.. *Financial Analysts Journal* 52, 47–56.

Kerkhof, J., Melenberg, B. and Schumacher, H. (2010). Model risk and capital reserves. *Journal of Banking and Finance* 34, 267–279.

Knight, F. (1921). *Risk, Uncertainty, and Profit.* Boston: Houghton Mifflin.

McNeil, A. J., Frey, R. and Embrechts, P. (2005). *Quantitative Risk Management.* Princeton Series in Finance. Princeton, NJ and Oxford: Princeton University Press.

Merton, R. (1969). Lifetime portfolio selection under uncertainty. *Review of Economics and Statistics* 51, 247–257.

Morini, M. (2011). *Understanding and Managing Model Risk: A Practical Guide for Quants, Traders and Validators.* Chichester: John Wiley & Sons.

Parkinson, M. (1980) The extreme value method for estimating the variance of the rate of return. *Journal of Business* 53(1), 61–65.

Rogers, L. C. G. and Satchell, S. E. (1991). Estimating variance from high, low and closing prices.. *Annals of Applied Probability* 1, 504–512.

Rösch, D. and Scheule, H., eds. (2010). *Model Risk.* London: Risk Books.

Satchell, S. and Christodoulakis, G., eds. (2008). *The Analytics of Risk Model Validation.* London: Academic Press.

Soklakov, A. N. (2010). Learning, investments and derivatives. Working Paper 1106.2882v1, arXiv.

(2013). Deriving derivatives. Working Paper 13047533v2, arXiv.

Spiegelhalter, D. (2014). The future lies in uncertainty. *Science* 345(6194), 264–265.

Talay, D. and Zheng, Z. (2002). Worst case model risk management. *Finance and Stochastics* 6, 517–537.

Tunaru, R. (2015). *Model Risk in Financial Markets*. Singapore: World Scientific.

Williams, D. (1999). Models vs. the market: Survival of the fittest. Report FIN514. New York: Meridien Research and Capital Market Risk Advisors (CMRA).

Yang, D. and Zhang, Q. (2000). Drift independent volatility estimation based on high, low, open and close prices. *Journal of Business* 73, 477–491.

Index

Printed in the United States
by Baker & Taylor Publisher Services

Printed in the United States
by Baker & Taylor Publisher Services